TALKSHEETS

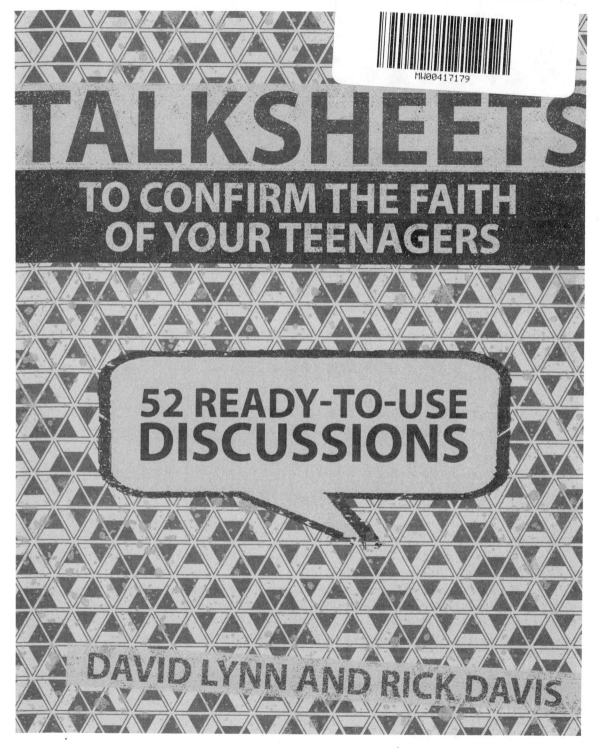

TO CONFIRM THE FAITH OF YOUR TEENAGERS

52 READY-TO-USE DISCUSSIONS

DAVID LYNN AND RICK DAVIS

ZONDERVAN.com/
AUTHORTRACKER
follow your favorite authors

YOUTH SPECIALTIES

TalkSheets to Confirm the Faih of Your Teenagers: 52 Ready-to-Use Discussions

Youth Specialties resources, 1890 Cordell Ct. Ste. 105, El Cajon, CA 92020 are published by Zondervan, 5300 Patterson Ave. SE, Grand Rapids, MI 49530.

ISBN 978-0-310-66873-2

Cover design by David Conn
Interior design by Brandi Etheredge Design

Printed in the United States of America

09 10 11 12 13 14 15 • 20 19 18 17 16 15 14 13 12 11 10 9 8 7 6 5 4 3 2 1

In great appreciation to our wives, Kathy Lynn and J.J. Davis, and our children, Amy Lynn and Megan Lynn, and Aaron Davis and Aurora Davis, and to our Christian brothers and sisters in the church universal.

CONTENTS

THE HOWS AND WHATS OF TALKSHEETS

CONFIRM IT! TalkSheets contain 50 discussions, each of which has a reproducible TalkSheet for your youth to work on, as well as simple, step-by-step instructions for how to use it. All you need are some Bibles, copies of the handouts inside these pages, and some kids (some food won't hurt, either). Then you're on your way.

These TalkSheets are user-friendly and very flexible. They can be used in youth group meetings, Sunday school classes, or in Bible study groups. You can adapt them for either large or small groups. And they can be covered in only a handful of minutes or explored more intensively over longer stretches. You can build an entire youth group meeting around a single TalkSheet, or you can use TalkSheets to supplement other materials and resources you might be covering.

IMPORTANT GUIDING PRINCIPLES BEFORE USING THESE TALKSHEETS

Let's begin by agreeing on two primary principles:

1. Faith is essentially caught not taught, and
2. The Holy Spirit alone works best to establish faith, changing someone from a knower to a believer and a church attendee to a lifelong follower of Jesus.

If we can agree on these principles, it's easier to explain how CONFIRM IT! is designed. It's not so much a teaching tool as a tool designed to engage real-faith connections and encourage faith vocabulary in young people.

Many church attendees don't know how to articulate their faith, nor do they often notice vital connections to their faith outside the church building. CONFIRM IT! TalkSheets are designed to help young people make connections between what they believe and their day-to-day lives, as well as develop a living faith vocabulary as opposed to a "church-speak" vocabulary used only in the "God building" to sound spiritual to adults and congregation leaders.

These CONFIRM IT! TalkSheets will help you engage young people in real conversations where belief can be discovered, Christian words and notions can be unpacked, and faith can be realized and expressed. In such settings the earliest Christians explored and expressed their faith. (For example, Jesus used fishing imagery as a jumping-off point to connect his first followers—fishermen—with what he was doing.) Creating similar settings for your group is essential.

WHY "CONFIRM"?

There is much expressed in the word *confirm* in this book's title. So often we fall into the trap of assuming we need to "make things happen" in young people. Nothing could be further from the truth—which is why we look to *confirm* faith, not *stuff it* or *cram it* down their throats. In faith we believe that God is at work in us already. Jesus promised the Holy Spirit would come to remind us and teach us (John 14:26).

There comes a time in the lives of young churchgoers when they need to find the skills to listen, make connections, and express faith in their own terms. We err if we believe a formal, public expression of faith is the only necessary expression. After all, we express our real faith in daily conversations, engaged moment to moment with the push and pull of "who is *your* Lord and Savior?" It's one thing when a teenager gives the expected, textbook answer; it's infinitely better for a youth to discover that Jesus comes as the answer in the midst of new, challenging settings such as school activities, malls, and parties.

Unless we assist our young people in discovering their faith and their own faith vocabulary, they will often find themselves mute in the face of challenges they encounter daily.

AN ENGAGING TOOL, NOT A TEACHING TOOL

Have you hammered down "obvious" answers to spiritual questions young people aren't even asking? Have you found yourself among young people who can answer your spiritual questions "correctly" but don't see why the answer is relevant to daily life?

Take, for example, the primary question of faith: "Who is your Lord and Savior?" The "right" answer is Jesus Christ. We have heard young people answer this question correctly for many years. But we have also witnessed young people stumped by what *Lord* means in a culture in which many are their own source of truth—and stumped as to why they must be saved when many believe they're basically okay. We often make the mistake of assuming good information is enough. But information is just the structure, the frame, on which youth must place vital, real-life experiences that will ultimately mature their faith.

And if we teach young people answers to questions they are not asking (or that they don't even know they need to ask), we leave them with answers that don't have any meaning or meat—and faith that won't survive life's challenges. This is why we believe young people need to understand the tensions of life from which questions arise—and that they must daily struggle with how they answer those questions in their lives, even before they hear how God has addressed those questions in the person of Jesus Christ. It's only then we can ask, "If this is how life is, then who is YOUR Lord and Savior?"

By engaging young people inwardly—what we like to call INNER-gizing them—into real dialogue about their lives and their perceptions and their faith, we can make pathways toward partnering with them as they grow in discipleship.

You may notice there are no "right" answers provided at the end of the book or on the leader's guide portion of each TalkSheet. Why? Because there *aren't* right answers to these questions. Again, this TalkSheet volume is not about getting young people to answer questions correctly. This may make some of you a little nervous. But this isn't a catechism; it's a collection of tools that can offer an avenue for young people to engage faith in their real lives.

Recently while using this material with a group of young people, we came to a question about a parable of two men who went to the temple to pray. I (Rick) asked, "What stands out for you in this story?" One young person spoke up quickly and, in his finest "church-ese," told me the "right" answer. Another gave me a similar answer. I stressed that there was no wrong answer here—just tell me what stands out for you. Then one young man said the most amazing thing: "I just don't get how this guy could be so dedicated to what he believed and have it so wrong." WOW! What a good insight! First, because it was an answer I hadn't heard before (likely since it was void of churchy expressions), and second, because it was a raw, unaffected insight that came right out of him. He made a personal connection to the parable.

A COMMON PITFALL TO AVOID

Faith development can be likened to a staircase with many steps. Some things need to be set in place before other things can be embraced. We might say that a person moves from A to B before moving on to C and eventually arriving at D. A mistake many leaders make is viewing the distance from A to D as short and simple to tackle; they're impatient with their charges, those who're supposed to be taking these steps in the manner and with the speed we deem acceptable. But good Christian leadership understands we are often guides or parts of larger encounters on the roadside as people make their way in following the Master.

Another pitfall common in Christian leadership is inviting people to make unsustainable leaps in faith development. So young believers often make a "substitutional" leap of faith, jumping from A to D based on what the leader tells them. They do this because they either trust their leaders way too much or are afraid to express doubts in an emotionally unsafe environment. They might also feel lacking and guilty.

In addition there's performance anxiety in our faith settings that can cause our young believers to take on language that fits the situation but is essentially not a part of their day-to-day lives. In other words...church-speak or Christian-ese.

Such followers attend gatherings but cannot pray for themselves, hold a secret sense of doubt and guilt, and often defer to the religious leadership on all matters of faith. Jesus compared such followers to shallow soil on which the seed falls.

YOUR ROLE AS THE LEADER

There are three roles a discussion leader can fulfill: An Instrument, a Thorn, or a Stage Director. An Instrument can be a force in the hand of the Holy Spirit who works in the process of faith building in the life of a young disciple. A Thorn can become an irritant in the life of disciples who alienates them from the faith community by creating an unsafe spiritual environment with unrealistic expectations and impatient discipleship methods. A Stage Director inoculates young people against catching real faith. How? By creating an environment that encourages satisfying expectations through wearing masks of believing and using language accepted by the church, effectively insulating them from embracing a real, vital faith expressed in a living language. As you can see, only one role serves well in the life of young followers—that of an Instrument.

The best discussions don't happen by accident. They require careful preparation and a sensitive and enthusiastic leader. Don't worry if you aren't experienced or don't have hours to prepare. TalkSheets are designed to help even the novice leader. The more TalkSheet discussions you lead, the easier the process becomes.

THESE TALKSHEETS HELP US BE GOOD STEWARDS OF A SACRED PROCESS

If we understand that deep, rich soil may take much mulching over a long period of time if a seed is to take root in it, then we leaders can trust that faith is not about "achieving" something in others' lives, but about the Holy Spirit shaping lives into that of followers. We can become stewards of a most sacred process. Young people can pick up useless notions of faith and life on their way to discovering real faith that rumbles deep within a vital discipleship. Patient and loving mentoring is needed if these useless notions are to be replaced with life-giving awareness in a living, vital faith in Jesus.

BEFORE LEADING A TALKSHEET SESSION

TalkSheets can be used as a curriculum for your youth group, but they're designed as springboards for discussion. They encourage your kids to take part and interact with each other. And hopefully they'll do some serious thinking, discover new ideas, defend their points of view, and make decisions.

Youth today live in an active world that bombards them with the voices of society and the media—most of which drown out what they hear from the church. Youth leaders must teach the church's beliefs and values—and help young people make the right choices in a world full of options.

A TalkSheet discussion works for this very reason. While dealing with the questions and activities on the TalkSheet, your kids will think carefully about issues, compare their beliefs and values with those of others, and make their own choices. TalkSheets will challenge your group members to explain and rework their ideas in a Christian atmosphere of acceptance, support, and growth.

Maybe you're asking yourself, *What will I do if the kids in my group just sit there and don't say anything?* Well, when kids don't have anything to say, a lot of times it's because they haven't had a chance to get their thoughts organized. Most young people haven't developed the ability to think on their feet. Since many are afraid they might sound stupid, they often avoid voicing their ideas and opinions.

The solution? TalkSheets let your kids deal with the issues in a challenging, nonthreatening way *before* the actual discussion begins. They'll have time to organize their thoughts, write them down, and ease their fears about participating. They may even look forward to sharing their answers! Most importantly, they'll want to find out what others say and open up to talk through the topics.

If you're still a little leery about a real discussion among your kids, that's okay! So keep the following tips in mind:

SET YOUR GOALS

TalkSheets are designed to move toward a goal, but you need to identify your goal in advance: *What would I like our youth to learn? What truth should our young people discover? What's the goal of the session?* If you don't know where you're going, it'll be hard to get there.

BE CHOOSY

Choose a TalkSheet based on the needs and maturity level of your group. Although some thought went into how the TalkSheets are organized in this book, don't feel obligated to use the TalkSheets in the order in which they appear. Use your best judgment and mix them up however your needs dictate—they are tools for you!

USE THE BIBLE

Most Christian adults believe the Bible has authority over their lives. It's not uncommon for them to start their discussions or support their arguments with Bible verses. But today's teenagers (even many Christian teenagers) form their opinions and beliefs from their own life situations first—then they decide how the Bible fits their needs. TalkSheets start with the realities of the adolescent world and then move toward the Bible. You'll be able to show them that the Bible can be their guide and that God does have something to say to them about their own unique situations.

TRY IT YOURSELF

Once you've chosen a TalkSheet for your group, answer the questions and do the activities yourself. (Though each TalkSheet session is similarly structured, they each contain different activities.) So imagine your kids' reactions to the TalkSheet—it'll help you prepare for the discussion and understand what you're asking them to do. Plus, you'll have some time to think of other appropriate questions, activities, and Bible verses that help tailor it to your kids.

GET SOME INSIGHT

On each leader's guide page, you'll find numerous tips and ideas for getting the most out of your discussion. You may want to add some of your own thoughts or ideas in the margins. And there's room to keep track of the date and the name of your group at the top of the leader's guide. You'll also find suggestions for additional activities and discussion questions.

There are some references to Internet links throughout the TalkSheets. These are guides for you to find the resources and information you need. For additional help, be sure to visit the Youth Specialties Web site (www.YouthSpecialties.com) for information on materials and further links to finding what you need.

MAKE COPIES

Your young people will need their own copies of the TalkSheet you're working on—but make sure you make copies of only the youth's side of the TalkSheet. The material on the reverse side (the leader's guide) is just for you. Remember: You can make copies for your group because we've said you can—but just for your group...not every youth group in your state! U.S. copyright laws haven't changed, and it's still mandatory to request permission before making copies of published material. Thank you for cooperating.

SET UP FOR THE DISCUSSION

Decide ahead of time if you'd like your young people to work on the TalkSheet individually or in groups. Make sure the seating arrangement is inclusive and encourages a comfortable, safe atmosphere for discussion. Theater-style seating (in rows) isn't discussion-friendly. Instead, arrange the chairs in a circle or semicircle (or sit on the floor with pillows!).

AT THE MEETING

INTRODUCE THE TOPIC

It's important to have a definite starting point to your session and introduce the topic before you pass out the TalkSheet copies to your group. Keep it short, to the point, and take care to avoid over-introducing the topic, sounding preachy, or resolving the issue before you've started. Your goal is to spark your youth's interest and leave plenty of room for discussion.

You can tell a story, share an experience, or describe a situation or problem having to do with the topic. You may want to jump-start the discussion by asking something like, "What's the first thing you think of when you hear the word ____________ [insert the word here]?" After a few answers, you can add something like, "Well, it seems we all have different ideas about this subject. Tonight we're going to investigate it a bit further..."

The following are excellent methods you can use to introduce any session in this book:

- Show a related short film or video.
- Read a passage from a book or magazine that relates to the subject.
- Play a popular CD that deals with the topic.
- Perform a short skit or dramatic presentation.

- Play a simulation game or role-play, setting up the topic.
- Present statistics, survey results, or read a newspaper article that provides recent information about the topic.
- Use an icebreaker or crowd game, getting into the topic.
- Use posters, videos, or any other visuals to help focus attention on the topic.

There are endless possibilities for an intro—you are limited only by your own creativity! Each TalkSheet offers a suggestion, but you're free to use any method with which you feel comfortable. But do keep in mind that the introduction is a very important part of each session.

THE OPENER

We've designed the OPENER to be a great kickoff to the discussion. (Some may work better before you pass out the TalkSheets; others may work better as discussion starters after your young people have completed their TalkSheets.) Check out the MORE section, too—it often contains an alternate opening idea or activity that'll help get young people upbeat and talking. TIP: When you're leading a game or OPENER, consider leading it like a game-show host. Now, that may not sound very spiritual, but when you think about what a game-show host does (builds goodwill, creates excitement, facilitates community, listens to others, etc.), it can sound pretty pastoral. Plus...it's more fun.

ALLOW ENOUGH TIME

Pass out copies of the TalkSheet to your kids after the OPENER and make sure each person has a pen or pencil and a Bible. There are usually four to six discussion activities on each TalkSheet. If your time is limited, or if you're using only a part of the TalkSheet, tell the group to complete only the activities you assign. Let them know how much time they have to complete the TalkSheet—and then again when there's a minute (or so) left. Go ahead and give them some extra time and then start the discussion when everyone seems ready to go.

SET BOUNDARIES

It'll be helpful to set a few ground rules before the discussion. Keep the rules to a minimum, of course, but let the kids know what's expected of them. Here are suggestions for some basic ground rules:

- **What's said in this room stays in this room.** Emphasize the importance of confidentiality. Confidentiality is vital for a good discussion. If your kids can't keep the discussion in the room, then they won't open up.
- **No put-downs.** Mutual respect is important. If your kids disagree with some opinions, ask them to comment on the opinions—not those expressing them. Personal attacks aren't kosher, and they detract from discussion.
- **There's no such thing as a dumb question.** Your group members must feel free to ask questions at any time. The best way to learn is to ask questions and get answers.
- **No one is forced to talk.** Some kids will open up, some won't. Let everyone know they have the right to pass or not answer any question.
- **Only one person speaks at a time.** This is a mutual respect issue. Everyone's opinion is worthwhile and deserves to be heard.

Communicate with your group that everyone needs to respect these boundaries. If you sense your group members are attacking each other or adopting a negative attitude during the discussion, do stop and deal with the problem before going on.

Remember that Thomas did not at first believe that Jesus was resurrected, even though the other disciples expressed to him what they'd witnessed. It is a great testimony to those early followers of Jesus that Thomas was still "in their midst" a week later when Jesus showed up and confirmed himself to Thomas—they didn't excommunicate him for his unbelief. Therefore it's important to create a safe environment where young people can explore their faith and express themselves without the expectation of answering "correctly," performing, or making a developmental leap they aren't ready to make as a disciple.

LEAD THE DISCUSSION

Encourage all your kids to participate. The more they contribute, the better the discussion will be.

If your youth group is big, you may divide it into smaller groups. Once the smaller groups have completed their discussions, combine the smaller groups into one large group and ask the different groups to share their ideas.

You don't have to divide the group with every TalkSheet discussion. Also, for some discussions, you may want to vary the group size or divide the youth into groups of the same gender.

The discussion should target the questions and answers on the TalkSheet. Go through them one at a time and ask the kids to share their responses. Have them compare their answers and brainstorm new ones in addition to the ones they've written down.

Always phrase your questions so you are asking for an opinion, not a be-all, end-all answer. The simple addition of the less threatening, "What do you think...?" at the beginning of a question makes it a request for an opinion rather than a demand for the right answer. Your kids will relax when they will feel more comfortable and confident. Plus, they'll know you actually care about their opinions, and they'll feel appreciated.

A WORD ABOUT USING THE AFRICAN BIBLE STUDY

The adapted African Bible Study you'll find in many of the discussions is a simple format designed to help your students learn how to go deeper relationally with a biblical text.

Developed by our Christian brothers and sisters in Africa, this method allows Scripture to engage us both corporately and personally. The key element is that it asks us to consider how we might live and act in response to what we've heard in God's Word rather than simply walking away with an idea from the Bible. Though the questions can seem individually directed, the value in the African Bible Study is that you're listening and responding as a group and can hear more than one voice.

Through continued use your group will become familiar with the process. After your teenagers have had a chance to explore the ABS individually, repeat it as a group. For each of the three steps, read the Scripture aloud, asking the students to listen and then respond to each step's question following a brief time of silence to allow your group to reflect upon the text.

While this process may seem awkward at first, your young people will grow familiar with this model of Bible study with repetitive use over time. As the facilitator of these discussions, avoid frustration if your young people do not seem to respond well at first. Familiarity with this approach will make the experience with Scripture deeper. By repetitively teaching your group this model of Bible study, through these discussions you will model for them a very helpful tool for lifelong discipleship, opening up a pattern for adult Bible study that engages spiritual growth.

AFFIRM ALL RESPONSES—RIGHT OR WRONG

Let your kids know that their comments and contributions are appreciated and important. This is especially true for those who rarely speak during group activities. Make a point of thanking them for joining in. This will be an incentive for them to participate further.

But remember that affirmation doesn't mean approval. Affirm even those comments that seem wrong to you. You'll demonstrate that everyone has a right to express ideas—no matter how controversial those ideas may be. If someone states an off-base opinion, make a mental note of the comment so you can discuss it with your young people later. Then in your wrap-up, come back to the comment or present a different point of view in a positive way. But don't publicly reprimand the young person who voiced the comment.

AVOID GIVING THE AUTHORITATIVE ANSWER

Some kids believe you have the correct answer to every question. They'll look to you for approval, even when they're answering another group member's question. If they start to focus on you for answers, redirect them toward the group by making a comment like, "Remember that you're talking to everyone, not just me."

LISTEN TO EACH PERSON

Good discussion leaders know how to listen. Although it's tempting at times, don't monopolize the discussion. Encourage others to talk first—then express your opinions during your wrap-up.

DON'T FORCE IT

Encourage all your kids to talk, but don't make them comment. Each member has the right to pass. If you sense the discussion isn't going well, go to the next question or restate the present question to keep things moving.

DON'T TAKE SIDES

Encourage everybody to think through various opinions and positions and then ask questions to get them going deeper. If everyone agrees on an issue, you can play devil's advocate by asking tough questions and stretching their thinking. Remain neutral—your point of view is your own, not your group's.

DON'T LET ANYONE (INCLUDING YOU) TAKE OVER

Nearly every youth group has one person who likes to talk and is perfectly willing to express an opinion on any subject—all the time. To counteract this, encourage equal participation from all members.

LET THEM LAUGH!

Discussions can be fun! Most of the TalkSheets include questions that'll make young people laugh and get them thinking, too.

LET THEM BE SILENT

Silence can be scary for discussion leaders—especially if they haven't led many of them. Some react by trying to fill the silence with a question or a comment. The following suggestions may help you handle silence more effectively:

- **Be comfortable with silence.** Let 30 seconds or so go by before you speak (which can feel like forever when you're leading a group). Then you may want to restate the question to give your kids a gentle nudge.
- **Talk about the silence with the group.** What does the silence mean? Do they really have no comments? Maybe they're confused, embarrassed, or don't want to share.
- **Answer the silence with questions or comments such as, "I know this is challenging to think about..." or, "It's scary to be the first to talk."** If

you acknowledge the silence, it may break the ice.

- **Ask a different question that may be easier to handle or that will clarify the one already posed.** But don't do this too quickly without giving your group time to think through the first one.
- **Use the "two more answers" key.** When you feel like moving on to the next question, you may want to ask for two more answers to the one you're finishing up—just to make sure you've heard all the young people's responses. This may help draw out young people who're more reluctant to share right away.

KEEP IT UNDER CONTROL

Monitor the discussion and be aware if it's going off track. This can happen quickly, especially if young people disagree or things get heated. Mediate wisely and set a positive tone. If a young person brings up an interesting side issue, decide whether or not to pursue it. If the discussion is going well and the issue is worth exploring, let them talk it through. But if things get way off track, say something like, "Let's come back to that subject later if we have time. Right now, let's finish our discussion on…" If your group seems bored with an issue, get them back on track with provocative questions you've prepared beforehand. Let the discussion unfold, but be sensitive to your group—especially regarding who is or isn't getting involved.

BE CREATIVE AND FLEXIBLE

If you find other ways to use the TalkSheets, use them! Go ahead and add other questions or Bible references. Don't feel pressured to spend time on every single activity. If you're short on time, you can skip some items. Stick with the questions that are the most applicable and relevant to your group.

BE THERE FOR YOUR KIDS

Some kids may want to talk more about a certain topic. (Hey, you got 'em thinking!) Let them know you can talk one-on-one after group time. Communicate to the kids that they can feel free to talk with you about anything—and confidentially. Let them know you're there for them with support and concern, even after the TalkSheet discussion has been completed.

CLOSE THE DISCUSSION

Present a challenge to the group by asking yourself, *What do I want my young people to remember most from this discussion?* There's your wrap-up! It's important to conclude by affirming the group and offering a summary that ties the discussion together.

Sometimes you won't need a wrap-up. You may want to leave the issue hanging and discuss it further in another meeting. That way your group can think about it more, and you can nail down the final ideas later. Either way, there's always a **Closing Prayer** at the end of each Leader's Guide that you can use with your kids no matter how you've chosen to use the material.

SECTION 1 QUESTIONS ABOUT CONFIRMING YOUR FAITH

If you declare with your mouth that Jesus is Lord, and believe in your heart that God raised him from the dead, you will be saved. **(Romans 10:9 ISV)**

Introduce the Topic

Allow Enough Time

AFFIRM ALL RESPONSES—RIGHT OR WRONG

Don't Be the Authoritative Answer

LISTEN TO EACH PERSON

Don't Force It

Don't Take Sides

LET THEM LAUGH!

Allow Silence

BE CREATIVE AND FLEXIBLE

Be There for Your Kids

TalkSheet #1

WHY "CONFIRM IT!"?

1. Read **Matthew 7:24-27.** Place a check mark in the box before the words or phrases you think describe characteristics of decisions built on sinking sand. Place an X in the box before the words or phrases you believe describe characteristics of decisions built on solid rock.

- ❒ Impulsive
- ❒ Caring and compassionate
- ❒ Self-centered
- ❒ Considering the consequences
- ❒ Inconsiderate
- ❒ Lazy
- ❒ Risky
- ❒ Thinking of others first
- ❒ Life-giving
- ❒ Greedy
- ❒ Entitled
- ❒ Thinking it through

2. Do you believe each of the following decisions are **R (building on solid rock)** decisions or **S (building on sinking sand)** decisions?

- ___ Pray daily for my friends
- ___ Ignore a new young person at school
- ___ Encourage a friend who has had a hard day
- ___ Help my little brother with his homework
- ___ Spread a rumor I've heard
- ___ Copy a friend's answers for homework I didn't do
- ___ Help at home without being asked
- ___ Use swear words to sound cool
- ___ Keep a ring I found at school
- ___ Volunteer to help with a Sunday school class

3. Being more attentive to Jesus would…

- ❒ Definitely help me make more solid rock decisions
- ❒ Neither help nor hurt my decision making
- ❒ Might help me make more solid rock decisions
- ❒ Not help me in the least make more solid rock decisions

4. Do you **A (agree)** or **D (disagree)** with each of these statements?

- ___ How I spend my time today has little impact on my future.
- ___ Important commitments in life are always changing.
- ___ Some of the most important decisions in life are made now.
- ___ When it comes to religion, it is best to check all options.
- ___ Good decisions today make for a stronger life tomorrow.

5. Finish these Sparkplug Sentences:

Deciding I believe in Jesus means I…

When I think about making a commitment to Jesus I think…

To say a relationship with Jesus is important to me would…

6. Read Matthew 13:44. What does this story have to do with you and Jesus?

1. WHY "CONFIRM IT!"?

THIS WEEK

Between ages 14 and 24, young people are bombarded with voices and claims from every direction. Those years are also when they make some of the most important decisions of their lives—such as making a faith commitment. We must help young people realize how important making this decision will be for their whole lives.

THE OPENER

Ask your group members to consider their lives in the future and draw a "verbal picture" of what they will be doing, what their families will be like, and what will be important to them when they turn 64 (after the Beatles song "When I'm 64"). Then ask, **Is there anything you need to do today to make sure that image is true tomorrow? How important are decisions you make today in relation to how you'll live tomorrow?**

DISCUSSION BY THE NUMBERS (Go through the TalkSheet one item at a time.)

1. How have you noticed people building their lives on sand? On rock? When have you done each of these?
2. Get a group consensus regarding R and S decisions. Ask, **What do R and S decisions have to do with our faith in Jesus Christ?**
3. Ask, **What do you think being more attentive to Jesus looks like?** Now see what this attentiveness has to do with R and S decisions. Examine those decisions with friends, family, school, self-image, and church. Ask, **Do we remain attentive to Jesus in each of these areas of life?**
4. Clear an area of the room and ask the group members to stand in the center. Designate an Agree side of the room and a Disagree side of the room. Then present each statement again, asking the young people to step to one side or the other of your meeting area depending on their answers. With each statement ask the young people to defend their answers.
5. Listen carefully to your group members' responses. Questions will arise from this activity that you can answer together with your group members.
6. Ask, **What do you think this verse has to do with you confirming your faith?**

CLOSING DISCUSSION

Read this statement: **Christians believe in a relationship with God through Jesus Christ. God establishes this relationship by working in us to make us aware of God and move us to desire that relationship. It is important we each make decisions for ourselves to live in response to what God has given us in Jesus.** Then ask your young people, **What does it mean to you to confirm YOUR faith in Jesus?**

CLOSING PRAYER

"Dear God, as we build our lives today—through the friendships we share, the interests we develop, the commitments we make—you ask us to consider seriously a commitment to be in relationship with you. You certainly have made a commitment to be with us in Jesus. Help us to realize how wonderful and important our own commitments to you can be. Amen."

TalkSheet #2

WHY I MUST "CONFIRM IT!"

1. Use the "What Makes Me ME?" Scale to rate the following items related to their importance in building your life.

1______2______3______4______5______
Nope Maybe Kinda

6______7______8______9______10______
Sure That's me!

a. My clothes
b. My after-school activities
c. My favorite music
d. My mom's/dad's job
e. My friends
f. My beliefs about life
g. My grades
h. My house

2. Read 1 Corinthians 3:10-11. Is Jesus Christ the foundation for your life, one of the rooms, or just a brick or two in the building of your life?

❒ Jesus is the foundation! ❒ Jesus is one of the rooms! ❒ Jesus is just a brick or two!

3. Finish these Sparkplug Sentences:

I think it is important in life to…

One thing I never want to lose in my life is…

In order to build my life on Jesus as the foundation, I need to…

4. List three ways you can tell something is very important to someone.

Way #1 ______________________________

Way #2 ______________________________

Way #3 ______________________________

5. Read Romans 10:8-11. Why do you think it is important to confirm your faith? What are some ways we can confirm our relationship with Jesus?

2. WHY I MUST "CONFIRM IT!"

THIS WEEK

The church asks its young people at a particular age to claim their own faith and affirm their own relationships with Jesus Christ. It is important that the church, rather than getting them to say the right words, assists them in coming to terms with key issues and questions, helping them see the relevance of a Christian faith and hope. When young people confirm their faith is a wonderful time to walk with them and help them ask the right questions—to help them understand the importance of affirming a faith in Jesus Christ in their own lives.

THE OPENER

This exercise is aimed at helping your young people explore what makes certain things important to them—are they building a solid life, or a life on unstable ground? And what does it mean to them to confirm their faith in Jesus? Begin by asking your young people to think about a few activities that are very important to them. Then have them choose one activity and ask, **Why is it important to you? How does it make you who you are?** This is designed to help your young people connect this session with their own life activities.

DISCUSSION BY THE NUMBERS (Go through the TalkSheet one item at a time.)

1. Allow time to discuss their answers, asking questions such as, How does that make you YOU? and, Why is that important for making you YOU?
2. Ask your group members to listen to 1 Corinthians 3:10-11 as you read it out loud. See how many of your group members gave the Sunday school answer of "Jesus is the foundation!" Talk together about what that looks like as well as what it might look like to make Jesus a room or a brick or two of the building of their lives.
3. These incomplete sentences are designed to get your young people thinking about what it means to give their lives to something—and if doing so will help them build strong lives.
4. Possible answers are that we notice others talking about certain subjects a lot, or we notice others spending a lot of time doing particular jobs or projects. Your young people may have other answers to offer. Give time to explore what people do when something or someone is important to them. Ask, How does this relate to making Jesus important in your life?
5. Explore the importance of confirming one's faith, not just as a young person, but throughout the developmental stages of life.

CLOSING DISCUSSION

Read the statement out loud and ask for your group's reaction: **Christians believe that a relationship with Jesus is something we need to have personally. There comes a time when each of us decides what and who we are going to have in our lives. When we commit our lives to another, we take that relationship personally. When God becomes real and personal to us, we can confirm our faith by recognizing our belief and stating it as a public affirmation: "Jesus Christ is MY Lord and Savior."** Ask, **If Jesus is important in your life, how will any of us know?**

CLOSING PRAYER

"Dear Jesus, we have heard about you and have been taught about you; and we know there comes a time when we will be asked what we believe and what is important to us. There are so many things and so many people that matter to us. We know that many of these will change as we grow but you will always be there in our lives. You ask us to have a relationship with you personally, and to do that, we know need to confirm that WE want to have a relationship with you. Help us to make a good decision—not just today, but every day of our lives. Amen."

And without faith it is impossible to please God, for whoever would approach him must believe that he exists and that he rewards those who seek him. **(Hebrews 11:6 NRSV)**

Introduce the Topic

Allow Enough Time

AFFIRM ALL RESPONSES—RIGHT OR WRONG

Don't Be the Authoritative Answer

LISTEN TO EACH PERSON

Don't Force It

Don't Take Sides

LET THEM LAUGH!

Allow Silence

BE CREATIVE AND FLEXIBLE

Be There for Your Kids

TalkSheet #3

HOW CAN I KNOW GOD?

1. **Gimme Five:** Find five things that can be known about the person who made this object by just examining it. Place an answer on each finger.

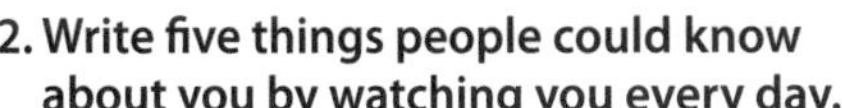

2. Write five things people could know about you by watching you every day.

a. ______________________
b. ______________________
c. ______________________
d. ______________________
e. ______________________

Write five things no one would know about you unless you tell them.

a. ______________________
b. ______________________
c. ______________________
d. ______________________
e. ______________________

3. Finish these **Sparkplug Sentences:**

One thing I can know about God by looking at what he has made is…

Something I can't know about God unless he tells me is…

One way God tells me about himself personally is through…

4. We Get 2 Know God 2 Ways

Natural revelation: (Name one way nature reveals something about God.)

Special revelation: (Name one thing only God could have revealed about himself through the Bible.)

5. What does John 1:18 tell us about knowing God?

No one has ever seen God, but God the One and Only, who is at the Father's side, has made him known. (NIV)

3. HOW CAN I KNOW GOD?

THIS WEEK

Young disciples need to understand that although God is big and complicated, God is knowable. One way to know God is through what God has made: Creation. But the knowledge we gain about God is incomplete if we know God through nature alone. It is through Jesus and through Scripture that God reveals to us what we need to know about him. In this week's session these two ways of knowing God, natural revelation and special revelation, are presented. Both notions are biblical and are presented most clearly in **Paul's letter to the Romans at 1:20** (natural revelation) and **John's Gospel at 1:18** (special revelation). This week's session will introduce the idea that God is knowable to us.

THE OPENER

In this exercise the young people will examine one object and offer five things they can clearly know about the person who made the object merely by examining the object. Select an object and place it where your group members can see it. Ask them to offer five things they can learn about the person who made it and write one on each finger of the hand outline from "1." The purpose of this exercise is to demonstrate that any created object discloses something about its creator. An object can be anything from a book, a pencil, a shoe, etc. What the young people know about the creator will be simple inferences. Try to push the group to come up with at least five knowable facts about the creator. Allow them two or three minutes to consider their five offerings.

DISCUSSION BY THE NUMBERS (Go through the TalkSheet one item at a time.)

1. Take time to let all your group members talk about how they know what they know. If they find it difficult, allow them to discuss the difficulty. It might be good here to offer your own five knowable aspects of the object's creator.

   Every created object tells us something about its creator. While in our culture we often do not look at objects as having a creator, it is important to experience that way of looking at the world around us. Ask, **Does everything that is created have a creator, and if so, does it naturally tell us something about its creator?**

   Challenge your group to consider something about an object's creator that is not knowable by examining the object alone, but can only be known if the creator tells us. What young people realize is that some things we can know by observation and some things we can know only if we are told. Take time to discuss these different ways of knowing.
2. Ask, **Do you think God is knowable in the same way?**
3. With the **Sparkplug Sentences**, the young people can enter into dialogue about the two ways God is revealed and knowable. Take time to allow each young person to respond to the sentences.
4. This activity presents the young people with two ways of understanding how God is revealed and made knowable. Allow each young person to offer his answer.
5. The Scripture verse from John's Gospel tells us that God, who has never himself been seen by anyone, is made knowable and "seeable" in Jesus.

No one has ever seen God, but God the One and Only, who is at the Father's side, has made him known.
John 1:18 (NIV)

CLOSING DISCUSSION

Christians believe that God is knowable in nature, called natural revelation (revealed naturally), but that that way of knowing God is incomplete. To really know God's heart, God's desire, and God's love we need God to tell us about himself by special revelation. We believe that Jesus is God's best and most perfect way of telling us about himself. Ask the group, **If we are going to know God, what gives us the clearest picture of God?**

CLOSING PRAYER

"Father, we would really like to get to know you in our lives. We see something of you in the created world around us and we know that you are powerful and good. Yet we long to know more of you. Thank you that you want us to know you, too, and that you speak to us about yourself in the words of the Bible. We hear and believe what the Bible tells us, that we can come to know you best of all through Jesus Christ our Lord. Amen."

TalkSheet #4

PSALM 23

A Song about God's Character

1. GIMME FIVE! Read Psalm 23 and quickly write five things David tells you about God's character.

1. ______________________________

2. ______________________________

3. ______________________________

4. ______________________________

5. ______________________________

2. Rate from most true to least true the following statements: Use letters A through F, with A being most true and F being least true. Place a letter by each statement.

_____ God is there to follow us all the way.
_____ With God we get what we want most of the time.
_____ Comfort comes from knowing God's presence.
_____ When hard times hit, God throws us a picnic.
_____ God tends us like a caring shepherd.
_____ A hard time is a godless place to be.

3. Finish these Sparkplug Sentences:

When I hear David's description of God, what strikes me most is…

If I wrote a song about God's character in my own words, I would begin "…

Because of David's psalm I know that…

4. Bible Echoes: Read Romans 8:38-39. **In what way does what Paul writes here echo what David wrote in Psalm 23:6?**

5. BOIL IT DOWN, DUDE!

If you could boil **Psalm 23** down to a single sentence, what is the message you are invited to live with every day?

4. PSALM 23: A Song about God's Character

THIS WEEK

Young people often wonder what God is really like. When we use "churchy" language to talk about God it can work to distance young people from a real sense of God's presence in their real lives. David's most famous psalm is a wonderful way for young people to explore the nature of God's character as seen through the eyes of a young boy who worked as a shepherd over his father's flock. Through everyday images that were familiar to him, David talks confidently about how he understands God in his life. Young people can find in David and his Psalm 23 an easy access into learning about God's character and also how to talk about what we know about God using the images of our own day-to-day lives.

THE OPENER

The purpose of this activity is to familiarize young people with a voice in the Old Testament and to explore how one can express experiencing God in a language that is familiar and relatable to their everyday world. The young people are asked to begin by looking at the lyrics of a song and discussing what that song tells them about life. Allow them two minutes to reflect on the lyrics of a song of your choice, either read quietly or spoken out loud, and consider what it tells them about life.

Take time to discuss what each young person hears about life in the song. Give the young people time to reflect on the question: **Is this a message you want to live with every day?** You might also ask, **What is the main point of the song? Are lyrics important? What might the song's lyrics tell you about the writer?**

Most song lyrics reflect what the writer believes. We often don't take the time to listen with young people and consider a song's message. Ask, **Are the lyrics helpful in understanding your world today?**

DISCUSSION BY THE NUMBERS (Go through the TalkSheet one item at a time.)

1. As you present Psalm 23, remind the young people this is a song written by a young David who worked as a shepherd. Challenge the group to list five things mentioned in Psalm 23 about God's character.
2. Ask the young people to consider which statements are true and which are less true. Using the letters A through F, have them place them in order with A being most true to F being least true. Allow time to discuss the reasons for their choices. Each of the statements can help you examine Psalm 23 through discussion.
3. Listen to the sentences as you answer questions that arise.
4. The Bible often has voices echoing each other. Paul, in writing to the church in Rome, closes his most powerful statements recorded in chapter 8 with a confidence that echoes David's. Invite the young people to consider how these two voices express similar thoughts with different wording.
5. Christians have always found ways to express the nature and the presence of God using the language of their own time. While David found a wonderful way to tell us of how he experienced God in his life, we can find ways today of expressing God. We believe God is knowable and that what we know of God can be expressed in ways we can all relate to. What we share with each other about God is something we can live with every day of our lives.

CLOSING DISCUSSION

David experienced the presence of God in his life and expressed what he came to know as the character of God by using images of the world he knew: A shepherd, pastures, a pool of water, a dark valley. Christians believe we can come to know God also, and understand God's character in ways familiar to us. God wants us to know him and know the comfort of his presence in all times and places. Ask your group, **How did David's words help you in your understanding about the character of God?**

CLOSING PRAYER

"Dear Father, Shepherd of our lives and Restorer of our souls, thank you for David's voice that tells us about your love and faithful presence. As he came to know you, may we, too, come to know you. Help us to find ways to speak of your love and your presence in our daily lives. Amen."

TalkSheet #5

GOD'S ATTRIBUTES

What Is God Like?

1. **Gimme Five** things people notice about you (or ***attribute*** to you).

    1. ______________________________
    2. ______________________________
    3. ______________________________
    4. ______________________________
    5. ______________________________

2. **Read 1 John 1:5.** What does John tell us that people have noticed about God or ***attributed*** to God?

3. Check which of the following attributes you think your friends have noticed about God:

___Eternal	___Faithful	___Gossipy	___Loud
___Stingy	___Loving	___Jealous	___Kind
___Omnipresent	___Hardheaded	___Patient	___Resentful
___Popular	___Conceited	___Merciful	___Raging

4. Finish these Sparkplug Sentences:

    Something I have noticed about God is…

    My personal favorite attribute of God is…

    An attribute of God's I would like people to also notice in me would be…

5. **Read Psalm 103:8-14.** What attributes of God are mentioned in this psalm? Which attribute stands out for you today as important?

5. GOD'S ATTRIBUTES: What Is God Like?

THIS WEEK

Young people want to know if God is knowable. Throughout Scripture we are told of specific aspects of God's character that are knowable and recognizable if we are to relate to God. We know that God is loving; that God is faithful and merciful. Young people need to learn that we can come to a better relationship with God when we learn more about God's character portrayed in the Bible. Through God's attributes we learn who God is to us and that we can count on God's faithfulness.

THE OPENER

Begin by asking your group members to consider what they think either their mom or dad was like at their age. Ask, **What do you think people first noticed when they saw your mom or dad when he or she was your age?**

DISCUSSION BY THE NUMBERS (Go through the TalkSheet one item at a time.)

1. We begin this session by asking the young people to consider what others notice about them. What people notice about them may be what people consider their attributes. Allow them ample time to consider five things people notice about them. Then invite them to share what they think others notice about them. You might ask if they feel what others notice about them to be true. Ask, **In what ways are the things people notice about you true to who you really are?**
2. Read aloud 1 John 1:5 and ask, **What does John tell us that people have noticed about God OR attributed to God?**
3. Ask the young people to place a check by the attributes that relate to God. Go over each attribute and ask, **How is this like or not like God? How true is this to what we know about God?**
4. These **Sparkplug Sentences** are designed to allow them to relate personally to the topic and create discussion.
5. See if there is one attribute that seemed to stand out for your group members.

CLOSING DISCUSSION

Christians believe that God is knowable. Through the ages people have noticed specific aspects of God's character, and we believe that God does not change his character but is faithfully consistent. We call these recognizable characteristics of God his attributes. We know we can learn to recognize God in our lives through his faithful attributes. Read 2 Timothy 2:11-13. When we consider God's attributes and that he will not "disown himself," what does that mean to you?

CLOSING PRAYER

"Dear Father, Lord of heaven and earth, we thank you that you are knowable to us. When we consider all your attributes, we each would like to thank you specifically for your ____________ [allow the young people to state one attribute of God for which they are thankful]. Truly, Father, we are thankful for who you are. Amen."

TalkSheet #6

WHAT'S IN A NAME?

(OR, Who God Isn't!)

1. On the "Now, *That* Gets Me Mad!" Scale, place the letter of each situation according to how much it would anger you.

1______2______3______4______5______
Who cares Wait a minute

6______7______8______9______10
How could you? OUCH!!

a. A classmate texts you, saying something about you that is not true.
b. Your teacher makes up an embarrassing pet name for you.
c. The person you are dating calls you by a past boy/girlfriend's name.
d. A relative forgets your name and keeps calling you by a cousin's name.
e. A friend on the phone slips and calls you by another friend's name.
f. Your dad calls you by a sibling's first name every time.

2. Read Exodus 20:1-7. What does God want us to know about him? Check each statement you agree with.

- That when it comes to being God, God is it!
- That God is selfish when it comes to our attention.
- That God is cool with what really matters to us.
- That God likes to have the weekend off, so keep it quiet down there!
- That God made everything and did it on purpose.
- That Bibles are expensive, so don't write in them. No, really!
- That who we say God is really matters to God.

3. A=Agree, D=Disagree. Circle A for agree and D for disagree.

a. What someone believes about God is her own business.	A	D
b. It is all the same God we all believe in.	A	D
c. The God in the Bible is particular in what he is and does.	A	D
d. It is important to know who God is and isn't.	A	D
e. As long as it is important to you, any belief in God is good.	A	D

4. Read 1 Kings 18:20-39. What was the big deal? Is there a difference between Baal and God?

5. Finish these Sparkplug Sentences:

I think who I understand God to be is…

One of the most important things I know about God is…

One thing I realize today about God is…

6. WHAT'S IN A NAME? (OR, Who God Isn't!)

THIS WEEK

In our present culture many different views of God are expressed and the current viewpoint of many young people is that each of us has a right to believe about God whatever we wish. But while they see that as true about God, it is another thing to experience misrepresentation of ourselves. Young people can learn that God is knowable and that his nature is not relative to anyone's viewpoint, but rather well expressed throughout the Bible.

THE OPENER

The opening activity asks your group members to remember a time they may have been misrepresented or called by a wrong name. Ask your group members to share a time when they called someone by a wrong name or perhaps when someone forgot their name and called them by another. Ask, **How does it feel to be called by a wrong name? How does feel if someone shares something about you that is not true?** This exercise encourages a discussion of how a name and an understanding of one's personhood are important. Explore the issue and the feelings of personal betrayal or embarrassment when a wrong name or identity is used. Ask, **Why is it important to be called by the correct name and know who you are?**

DISCUSSION BY THE NUMBERS (Go through the TalkSheet one item at a time.)

1. Ask the young people to consider each situation and how it may make them feel by placing the corresponding letter on the "**Now, *That* Gets Me Mad!**" Scale. Allow enough time for them to discuss each situation and how it might make them feel.
2. Why is it important to know who God is and who God is not? Ask everyone to listen to the Bible reading and then consider the seven statements in regard to which would seem important to God for us to know.
3. These Agree/Disagree sentences are designed to increase discussion on the topic of knowing who God is and who God is not. Allow the young people time to answer and then share their answers.
4. Ask your young people to listen to the Bible reading and determine what was the big deal. Isn't God by any name still God? Or is there something important here that we learn about God from this reading? The important notion for your group to discover is that who God is and how God acts are not for us to determine. It matters who we worship as God. Baal was someone's notion of who God is, but as we find out in this reading, that notion of who God is was not God. It matters to God that we know who God is and that we not fill in the gaps with our own imaginations. The Bible is the best record of encounters with God that can offer a good picture of who God is. It is only in Jesus that God makes himself truly knowable.
5. Ask the young people to finish the incomplete sentences. Answer questions that arise from these sentences.

CLOSING DISCUSSION

Christians believe that God is knowable and that there are specific aspects of God that are important to know about his character that are found in Scripture and in Jesus. In Jesus we see and come to know clearly what God is like. Since God is knowable, then that nature of God is not relative to our varied viewpoints. God wants us to know him and not to misrepresent him. Ask, **Do you feel God has a specific personality like you, and is it important to know him as he really is?**

CLOSING PRAYER

"Dear Father, Creator of all that is, you have expressed yourself to us down through the ages. You have made it clear who you are and who you are not. You have said that knowing who you are matters to you and to us. Help us draw near to Jesus that we may come to know you better in our lives. Amen."

TalkSheet #7

WHAT IS THE TRINITY?

1. Consider something in your world that is one thing and yet seems like different things in varied situations or conditions. How can these things act like more than one?

❒ Water
❒ Chocolate
❒ Flour
❒ Sugar
❒ Light
❒ Wood

2. Read John 1:1-2, 14. What is John telling us about the Word and God? Who is this **Word** who became flesh?

3. GIMME FIVE: One person can wear "different hats" in different situations and relationships. Pick one person in your life and list the five different people they can be.

1. ______________________________
2. ______________________________
3. ______________________________
4. ______________________________
5. ______________________________

4. Listen to John 14:23-26. List three characteristics that make—

God the Father __________ __________ __________

God the Son __________ __________ __________

God the Spirit __________ __________ __________

5. Finish these Sparkplug Sentences:

When I think that God relates to us as three persons, it makes me wonder…

When I think of God as Father, I know that…

If I am given the Holy Spirit to comfort and guide me, I want to…

7. WHAT IS THE TRINITY?

THIS WEEK

One of the foundational principles of faith in God is that God is one and that there is no other. At the same time Scripture alludes to God as Father, Son, and Holy Spirit—three in one. While it is an essential concept and common in the language of the church, it can be very confusing for young and old alike. The Trinity is a complex concept the church has grappled with for centuries. This session invites the young people to consider the Trinitarian nature of God and encounter some of the scriptural language.

THE OPENER

Read the following riddle to your group:

You can walk on me, build with me, and many on me play.
I can swallow you whole, spit you up, and clean
your clock today. Still, I satisfy like no other and hide
in your next breath.

Ask, **What am I?** Most likely your group members will come to an answer of "water" quickly. By looking at the riddle itself you invite them to consider how water can take different shapes and be experienced differently while still remaining in essence water. The primary concern of this exercise is the discussion of the description more than the answer.

Allow ample time for the young people to come up with the riddle's answer and then explore the riddle's description with them. It is important to have them consider how water can not only take three or more distinct forms—solid (ice, snow), liquid, gas—but also how we relate to it differently in these different forms. It is the relational aspect that is of primary importance when we consider the Trinity.

DISCUSSION BY THE NUMBERS (Go through the TalkSheet one item at a time.)

1. Ask the young people to consider something that might display different qualities or characteristics in different settings or situations. Allow time for them to offer two or three examples for each item listed. Then ask, **How can one thing act like more than one?**
2. Have the young people read John 1:1-2, 14. These verses contain a complex idea John tries to express about God and the Word by saying the Word WAS WITH God and at the same time WAS God. Ask, **What do you think about the way John expresses this idea?** Then ask, **What is John telling us about the Word and God? Who is this Word who became flesh?** Answer: Jesus.
3. This **GIMME FIVE** activity asks the young people to come up with a person in their lives who performs differently or has different relationships due to different situations or conditions. An example might be a father who is also a son, husband, banker, ballplayer, shopper, etc. Explore how in different ways the one person can relate differently in each role.
4. An example could be God as the Father "created the world" or God the Son "walked with the disciples and ate with them." Allow ample time for the young people to consider how God relates to us practically in these three expressions of his presence.
5. Questions will arise from these sentences that you can answer together as a group.

CLOSING DISCUSSION

Christians understand God to be one God, and there is no other. And at the same time we experience God as the Creator and Giver of all life, as the Word made flesh in Jesus, and as the power and presence of God in the Holy Spirit. The Bible speaks of God as one and yet in practical terms we are told of God the Father, Son, and Holy Spirit. We are told to baptize in the name of all three (Matthew 28:18-20), yet to understand it is only one God in whose name we live and witness. God expresses himself to us in a depth of relationships that can only be expressed in the Trinity. Ask, **How does the Trinity of God help you have a greater relationship with God?**

CLOSING PRAYER

"Dear Lord God, Father, Son, and Holy Spirit, you have expressed yourself to us in such wonderful and amazing ways. And yet in all these ways it is still you and you alone who is God. Thank you for creating us, Father. Thank you for walking with us in flesh and redeeming us, Jesus. Thank you for strengthening us and guiding us daily, precious Holy Spirit. Thank you, Lord God, for coming to us in ways we need to bring us always and in all ways to you. Amen."

SECTION 3 QUESTIONS ABOUT JESUS

There is salvation in no one else, for there is no other name under heaven given among mortals by which we must be saved. **(Acts 4:12 NRSV)**

Introduce the Topic

Allow Enough Time

AFFIRM ALL RESPONSES—RIGHT OR WRONG

Don't Be the Authoritative Answer

LISTEN TO EACH PERSON

Don't Force It

Don't Take Sides

LET THEM LAUGH!

Allow Silence

BE CREATIVE AND FLEXIBLE

Be There for Your Kids

1. Consider the following "Witnesses." Place the letter of the witness on the "Credibility" Scale according to the reliability of the witness to a bank holdup.

I______2______3______4______5______
Not so credible Somewhat

6______7______8______9______10______
Better than most Very credible

a. A teller at the window of the bank across town
b. A customer in the bank getting a loan
c. A passing policeman who gets the call to the bank
d. The teller in the bank at the time of the robbery
e. The robber
f. A mother with three children getting in her car in front of the bank

TalkSheet #8

JESUS

The Last WORD on God

2. A=Agree, D=Disagree. After reading John 1:18 agree or disagree with the following statements. Circle A for agree and D for disagree.

There are many ways to get a sense of what God is like.	A	D
It is not really possible to know clearly what God is like.	A	D
Jesus is all about giving us a clear sense of what God is like.	A	D
To get to know what God is like I need to study the Bible.	A	D
What God is thinking about us is anyone's guess.	A	D

3. Finish these Sparkplug Sentences:

Jesus shows what God is like when he…

Something about Jesus that makes God very clear to me is…

What John is telling me about Jesus is…

4. Gimme Five things that Jesus shows us about God:

1. ______________________________

2. ______________________________

3. ______________________________

4. ______________________________

5. ______________________________

5. What's that you say? Read John 14:8-11 and look at Jesus speaking to Philip about himself. In your own words, what is Jesus trying to get across to Philip?

8. JESUS: The Last WORD on God

THIS WEEK
In our culture many voices are clamoring for a young person's attention, and there are many voices that claim to tell us what God is like. The Bible makes it clear that only Jesus gives us a clear representation and makes God knowable to us. In Scripture God is most clearly seen through his Son.

THE OPENER
This activity introduces some of the voices in today's culture that compete for the eyes and ears of young people. Ask for volunteers to play the following "voices":

- Pop music
- Magazine advertising
- Mom or Dad
- Popular television programming
- Jesus
- Social networking Internet sites such as Facebook

Ask another volunteer to play the "average" young person, who then stands in the middle of your group with the other six "voices" around him or her. The voices are given 30 seconds to present their message simultaneously to the "average" young person standing in their midst. At the end of the 30 seconds, ask the "average" young person what it was like to have so many voices vying for his or her attention. Ask, **Did you treat each of the voices the same?**

DISCUSSION BY THE NUMBERS (Go through the TalkSheet one item at a time.)

1. The purpose of this activity is to help your young people consider the Bible's claim that Jesus is the voice and presence through which we can best come to know God. We begin by exploring who might be a best witness—someone we would listen to who would have the best way of knowing the truth and telling the truth. Allow your young people to consider each witness and place the corresponding letter on the "Credibility" Scale from least credible to most credible. See how your young people placed their values, giving them each time to tell why they felt the witness was more or less credible. Remember to have them consider who might know the truth and also tell the truth. Each young person may have different viewpoints, so allow time to explore their perspectives.
2. Ask, **Are there many ways to know God, or is Jesus the only way? Do we get a better sense of Jesus by studying the Bible?**
3. Open a discussion using the three **Sparkplug Sentences** about the nature of Jesus and what we come to know of God because of Jesus. You might want to record the responses everyone had in common on flipchart paper or a whiteboard. Ask, **How do you think Jesus coming in the flesh helped people better understand more about God?**
4. Ask the young people to offer five things they now know about God because of Jesus. **Do we know God better now because of how Jesus has made him known? What can we know today about God through Jesus that people living in Old Testament times would not have had the privilege of knowing because Jesus had not yet been come to earth?**
5. Have the young people use their own wording to say what Jesus is telling Philip.

CLOSING DISCUSSION
Christians believe that Jesus is the clearest presentation of the heart and desire of God. He is "the WORD," or "the meaning," that has taken on flesh and walks in our world as one of us. In Jesus, God comes to us to let us know him. We can know what the Father is like, how he cares about us, and how he wants us to relate to him and to each other. In Jesus, God has made himself knowable. Ask your group, **What is one thing about God that Jesus has made known to you that you will never forget?**

CLOSING PRAYER
"Dear Father, we could never really know you unless you made yourself knowable to us. But you want us to know you. And in Jesus you have made yourself knowable. Help us draw nearer to Jesus that we might know you better. Amen."

TalkSheet #9

INCARNATION

1. **GIMME FIVE Plus FIVE:** List five characteristics of God and of human beings.

GOD: ____________________
____
____
____
____

HUMAN: ____________________
____
____
____
____

Consider: In what ways was Jesus distinctly both at the same time?

2. **Read John 1:14. What three things stand out for you that you could tell someone else about Jesus because of this verse?**

3. **Finish these Sparkplug Sentences:**

God in the flesh (incarnation) means to me that…

What is important to me about the incarnation is…

What confuses me about the incarnation is how…

4. **Share two incidents you remember from the Bible—one demonstrating that Jesus is God and one demonstrating that Jesus is human.**

Jesus is God story: ______________________________

Jesus is human story: ______________________________

5. **African Bible Study – Read Hebrews 2:14-18 three times, stopping each time to reflect.**

1st Reading – What stands out to you?

2nd Reading – How does this connect with your world?

3rd Reading – What do you feel called to do in response?

9. INCARNATION

THIS WEEK

The incarnation is essential to our Christian understanding and is at the same time a great mystery. We affirm the truth of the incarnation and yet cannot claim to understand how it is true. Certainly it is presented in Scripture. Young people may be confused about the incarnation, feeling that it means Jesus was some kind of superman, or they may feel that we need to be able to prove the reality of this mystery. This session is designed to engage your young people in a conversation about the incarnation that can engage them with the power of God with us.

THE OPENER

Begin by asking, **In what way are your parents visible and present in you?** Answers will vary depending on the family traits evidenced in us. Remember that this line of discussion may be difficult for adopted youth or youth in a foster care system. Be sensitive to this and remind everyone that the families we live with often have traits that brush off on us and become a part of our character—that make us who we are and how we behave.

When everyone is ready, ask them to share. Be sensitive to feelings, yet encourage everyone to notice how our families make a clear, noticeable impression on us. Explore with the young people how this is so. Ask, **How might Jesus also reflect his family in who he is and how he acts?**

DISCUSSION BY THE NUMBERS (Go through the TalkSheet one item at a time.)

1. Ask your young people to make two lists containing five characteristics of God and five characteristics of a human being. When they have finished their responses, ask them to share and compare. Then ask them to consider in what ways Jesus distinctly demonstrated both sets of characteristics at the same time.

   Possible answers:

   GOD—Love, Spirit, Truth, Knows everything, All-powerful

   HUMAN—Emotional, Needs to eat and sleep, Gets tempted, Joy, Gets hurt

2. Listen to all the things your group members could tell someone else about Jesus because of this verse. Choose the top three.
3. Ask your group members to finish the incomplete sentences. Then talk about their questions regarding God in the flesh. If you don't know the answer, say so.
4. Ask the young people to share two incidents they remember in which one demonstrated that Jesus is God, and the other demonstrated that Jesus is human. Example of God—stories of Jesus healing the blind. Example of humanity—Jesus being hungry, tired, or crying.
5. Explore Hebrews 2:14-18 using the African Bible study.

CLOSING DISCUSSION

Christians believe that the incarnation is God with us in a vulnerable, physical, and personal presence we know as Jesus. How God did this is a mystery, but the fact that Jesus is God's real presence with us was settled when the first believer recognized him as "Lord," a title only reserved for God himself. All the writers in the New Testament express that Jesus was clearly human and yet at the same time the very distinct presence of the living God. Ask, **What is important to you about the incarnation in your Christian experience? How tough is it to believe in Jesus as God in a body?**

CLOSING PRAYER

"Dear Father, the Bible tells us you have come to us in the most personal way possible, wrapped in flesh and bone, reaching out to us in the words, deeds, and presence of Jesus. We believe that to know Jesus is to know you, because Jesus is your most personal expression to us of your mind and heart. While we don't really understand how this could be, we thank you that it is true and that in Jesus you come as one of us to be knowable to us. Amen."

TalkSheet #10

THE RESURRECTION

Part 1

1. Rate the following on the "Personal Worst Loss" Scale.

I______2______3______4______5______
No big deal

6______7______8______9______10
Big loss

a. You lose your car keys on a collector key chain.
b. You lose the concert tickets to see your favorite band.
c. Your best friend moves far away.
d. Your pet dies.
e. You grow out of your favorite outfit.
f. Your house burns down.

2. Read John 11:17-27. What would you say to Jesus if you were standing with Martha at this moment? What would you say to Martha?

3. A=Agree, D=Disagree. Consider the following statements and decide if you agree or disagree. Circle A for agree and D for disagree.

We should all accept death as a natural part of living.	A	D
Death is nature's way of keeping down the population.	A	D
Death is an enemy to be defeated.	A	D
Eat, drink, and be merry because tomorrow we die.	A	D
Death is an enemy of God's creation.	A	D

4. Finish these Sparkplug Sentences:

What confuses me about the resurrection is…

I find comfort in the resurrection in that…

If I could ask God one thing about the resurrection it would be…

5. African Bible Study – Read John 11:32-44 three times, stopping each time to reflect.

1st Reading – What stands out to you?

2nd Reading – How does this connect with your world?

3rd Reading – What do you feel called to do in response?

10. THE RESURRECTION: Part 1

THIS WEEK

Death is a harsh reality most young people (as well as adults) have a hard time encountering. The media and culture offer many mixed and confusing images of death. The resurrection—and the hope it brings to Christians—stands in stark contrast to death and is essential to our Christian hope and understanding. Life after death is not a mechanism fixed into nature, but rather an intentional act of God to raise us from the dead and restore us to life in his presence. The story of Lazarus demonstrates the heartache of death as a human tragedy and the power of God to conquer death through Jesus.

THE OPENER

Begin by asking your young people to share a time they encountered death. When all are ready, have them share their encounter. Validate every real encounter with death from the smallest and seemingly insignificant to the most personal. Death in this world is everywhere and any encounter tells us something about the nature of death. Ask, **What stands out for you in this encounter with death?**

DISCUSSION BY THE NUMBERS (Go through the TalkSheet one item at a time.)

1. Ask your group members to share their lowest-rated losses and their highest-rated. Ask, **Why did you rate this one lowest and why did you rate this one highest?** Talk about the frequency of losses we have and will experience throughout life. To be born into this world is to be born into a world of grieving over losses (pets, boyfriends/girlfriends, loved ones).
2. Listen to the responses of your group members. Ask, **How many of your friends do you think believe in a resurrection at the end of time?**
3. See commentary in bold after each statement.
   - We should all accept death as a natural part of living. **Death isn't natural but is a result of the fall from God. We were created to live in eternity with God but the sin of humankind doomed us to death.**
   - Death is nature's way of keeping down the population. **Deaths that result from plagues, famines, and wars have lowered the population but death is the result of evil. When sin entered the world so did death (see Romans 5:12; 1 Corinthians 15:22).**
   - Death is an enemy to be defeated. **The "payoff" for sin is death, but fortunately for us, there is life through Jesus Christ (see Romans 6:23).**
   - Eat, drink, and be merry because tomorrow we die. **Ecclesiastes 8:15, looking at the emptiness of life, concludes this. But we have a purpose for living beyond seeking pleasure (see Ephesians 2:10).**
   - Death is an enemy of God's creation. **Yes, in the sense that death is the result of sin. But Christ conquered death (see 1 Corinthians 15:54). Even though everyone must die because of sin, those who have placed their faith in Christ will live again.**
4. This is an opportunity for you to answer questions about resurrection. **Don't be afraid to say, "I don't know" if you don't.**
5. Remind the young people how to do an African Bible study. **You will read the text slowly, asking them to respond after each reading to the provided question. This exercise draws the young people deeper into the Scripture and paves the way for a spiritual discipline with Scripture in the future.**

CLOSING DISCUSSION

Christians believe that Jesus has conquered death. An important part of the Christian experience is that we trust our lives and the lives of those we love to him in the hope he will raise us all from the dead and that death will be no more. Yet it is also part of the Christian experience to suffer loss when a loved one dies and we remain without them in this world. The weeping for a loved one is validated when Jesus himself joins Mary in tears at the death of Lazarus. So we view death as tragedy and triumph, defeat and yet victory, because of Jesus. Ask, **What is one thing you will want to remember about Lazarus being raised from the tomb? What do you think about the Christian view of death?**

CLOSING PRAYER

"Dear Father, death has a real power in our lives. If not for you and the Good News of life eternal through the power of the resurrection, our lives would be lived for this moment only. But we hear we can have hope and be lifted out of fear and dread into peace and comfort because Jesus has risen from the dead. And because he lives, we will live also. Thank you for this incredible Good News, Father. Amen."

TalkSheet #11

THE RESURRECTION

Part 2

1. **GIMME FIVE** things that stand out to you when you think about death.

 1. ______________________________

 2. ______________________________

 3. ______________________________

 4. ______________________________

 5. ______________________________

2. **Read John 20:1-18.** What strikes you most in this reading? If you were there with Mary Magdalene what would you have done?

3. Finish these **Sparkplug Sentences:**

 The important thing about the resurrection to me is…

 Knowing Jesus rose from the dead means that…

 Because of the resurrection I can…

4. **Face Off:** Offer three things about death that trouble you and three things about the resurrection that comfort you.

Trouble		Comfort
____________	/	____________
____________	/	____________
____________	/	____________

5. **African Bible Study** – Read **Romans 8:35-37** three times, stopping each time to reflect.

 1st Reading – What stands out to you?

 2nd Reading – How does this connect with your world?

 3rd Reading – What do you feel called to do in response?

11. THE RESURRECTION: Part 2

THIS WEEK

The resurrection of Jesus is perhaps the pinnacle of the expression of God's power to reign in the lives of his people. In our culture there is a great deal of pressure to downplay this historical demonstration of the Good News of Jesus and to explain it away as a non-event. But for Christians the resurrection of Jesus is essential to the Christian hope. As Paul tells us in 1 Corinthians 15:17, *"And if Christ has not been raised, your faith is futile..."* The resurrection of Jesus is the cornerstone of our hope and faith in Christ.

THE OPENER

Read the following statements out loud to your group:

"She's in a *dead-end* job."
"He has an important *deadline* coming up."
"They're at the *end of their rope.*"
"Life is filled with *little deaths.*"
"That is *the final curtain.*"

Decide together what each of the statements means. Ask, **When would you use each of these statements? In what ways do these statements relate to death?**

DISCUSSION BY THE NUMBERS (Go through the TalkSheet one item at a time.)

1. Ask the young people to list five things that stand out for them when they think about death. Remember: Since death is a tough topic, young people may choose some fun answers as well as serious to deal with the topic.
2. Ask, **If Jesus has the power to raise people from the dead, what does that say about Christianity? Do you believe that you, too, will be resurrected after you die?**
3. Listen to your group's completed sentences. Don't immediately correct any theological errors in your group members' responses. Rather, ask probing questions to help them get to the truth themselves.
4. Allow a few minutes for the young people to offer their responses and then have them present their responses in a face-off manner: *"What troubles me about death is ____________, and what comforts me in death is ____________."* When they are finished, ask them to choose which side they wish to give their support.

   Let your group members share both the troubling things about death and the comforting things about life. Ask an obvious question: **Which side of the equation gives you courage to live life for Christ?**
5. The African Bible study is a great way to look at **Romans 8:35-37.**

CLOSING DISCUSSION

Christians believe that Jesus has conquered death. An important part of the Christian experience is that we trust our lives and the lives of those we love to him in the hope he will raise us all from the dead and that death will be no more. Yet it is also part of the Christian experience to suffer loss when a loved one dies and we remain without them in this world. That's why Mary Magdalene is weeping at the tomb of Jesus. Ask, **What is one thing you will want to remember about Jesus being raised from the tomb? What do you think about the Christian view of death?**

CLOSING PRAYER

"Dear Father, death has a real power in our lives. If not for you and the Good News of life eternal through the power of the resurrection, our lives would be lived for this moment only. But we hear we can have hope and be lifted out of fear and dread into peace and comfort because Jesus has risen from the dead. And because he lives, we will live also. Thank you for this incredible Good News, Father. Amen."

TalkSheet #12

JESUS AS SAVIOR

1. A=Agree, D=Disagree. Circle **A** for agree and **D** for disagree.

a. Jesus came to teach us a better way to live.	A	D
b. Jesus' main ministry was to demonstrate an obedient life.	A	D
c. Jesus came to pull the wreckage of humanity from the fire.	A	D
d. Jesus offers us a way to be saved.	A	D
e. Jesus is God's answer to our daily troubles.	A	D
f. Jesus saves us from ourselves.	A	D

2. Consider, Choose, and Discuss what it means to "save" something on a computer or in an electronic game.

- ❒ You keep what you have done up to this point.
- ❒ No one else can see what you have done.
- ❒ Something is kept from being lost.
- ❒ Something is now held in a special safe place.
- ❒ From now on you start from this place.
- ❒ No one can stop you now—ha, ha.
- ❒ The Force is indeed with you, young Jedi.

3. DIG into 1 Timothy 1:15 for three things in this text you believe God really wants YOU to know…

____

____

____

4. Finish these Sparkplug Sentences:

"Jesus is Savior" to me means that…

Something I believe I need to be saved *from* is…

Something I believe I need to be saved *to* is…

If Jesus is my Savior, I need to…

5. GIMME FIVE things you witness in our world that demonstrate we need a Savior.

1. ______________________________ 2. ______________________________

3. ______________________________ 4. ______________________________

5. ______________________________

6. Read to Acts 4:5-12 and consider: If you had been present to hear Peter speak, what would have stood out for you in his manner and in his words?

12. JESUS AS SAVIOR

THIS WEEK

Young people are asked to profess their faith in Jesus by stating that Jesus is their Savior. To say that Jesus is your Savior means you determine and agree that you need to be saved *from* something and *to* something. In our current culture we should not take it for granted that we all understand this nature of Christ's work in our world. This session creates an opportunity to discuss the nature of Jesus as Savior in our lives.

THE OPENER

Begin by asking the group the following question: **If you were asked by your school to decide which classes should be cut from the curriculum and which should be saved, which would you save?**

DISCUSSION BY THE NUMBERS (Go through the TalkSheet one item at a time.)

1. We begin by asking the young people to consider statements about Jesus and determine if they agree or disagree with the statements. An important aspect of this kind of exercise is that people may agree or disagree for different reasons or different perceptions of a statement. Take time to explore with two or three the reasoning behind their responses.
2. Ask your young people to consider what it means when you save something on a computer or in a computer game by choosing and discussing two most likely answers from those provided. Then ask, **In what ways is this like what it means to be "saved" by Christ?**
3. Write down your group members' responses on flip-chart paper or a whiteboard. See which responses were unique and which the group held in common.
4. Notice in this set of questions that numbers 2 and 3 ask them to consider what they are saved "from" (selfishness, pride, sin) and what they are saved "to" (a new life in Christ, a life of purpose and meaning in Christ, eternal life).
5. Listen to your group members' responses. Talk about this as evidence of the sinful world in which we live versus the unbiblical view that people are innately good. The truth—people do sin and do need a Savior to deliver them from the ultimate consequence of death resulting from this sin.
6. Ask, **Why do you think the disciples were so passionate about telling others Jesus has the power to save? How excited are you about Jesus' saving power?**

CLOSING DISCUSSION

Christians believe we need a Savior and that Jesus Christ is the means through which our sins are forgiven, our brokenness is mended, and real reconciliation is established in our relationship with God. Where the law of God was unable to save us because it was weakened by our sinful nature, God worked in Jesus to establish a way and a means by which we are saved from our fallen state and restored to a right relationship with God. Ask, Why do you think is it important in the Christian experience to understand and affirm that Jesus is your Savior?

CLOSING PRAYER

"Dear Lord Jesus, you came into our world and our lives to remove the ugly stain of sin and self-centered living and to give us again this wonderful relationship with God. Thank you for loving us enough to pull us from the 'wreck' of our lives. Thank you for saving us from sin and saving us to a new life filled with hope. Amen."

TalkSheet #13

JESUS IS LORD

1. **Gimme Five** things that make a person an authority worth listening to in your life:

    1. ______________________________
    2. ______________________________
    3. ______________________________
    4. ______________________________
    5. ______________________________

2. Read **Matthew 8:23-27.** In what ways does this story illustrate that Jesus is someone who has great authority? (Check those answers with which you agree.)

    - ❒ He sang all the cool pirate songs while on the boat.
    - ❒ Jesus always caught the most fish while out on the lake because he was an authority on fishing.
    - ❒ He showed he could sleep through anything.
    - ❒ He did something no human could do.
    - ❒ Christ was fearless.

3. Rate the following people in your life on the "Trustworthy Authority" Scale:

    I_______2_______3_______4_______5_______6_______7_______8_______9_______10

    None Some Will listen to Real authority

    a. Another teenager who sits behind you
    b. A traffic policeman
    c. A brother or sister
    d. A coach
    e. Mom and Dad
    f. A close friend

4. Finish these **Sparkplug Sentences:**

    A person I listen to needs to be someone who…

    What clearly makes Jesus my Lord is that he…

    For me to follow Jesus as my Lord, I need to…

5. Read **Luke 6:46-49.** What does Jesus tell us about his Lordship in our lives? (Check those answers with which you agree.)

    - ❒ We must choose to make Jesus our Lord.
    - ❒ It's not enough to just say Jesus is Lord.
    - ❒ Obedience is a big part of Lordship.
    - ❒ You can't live near a sandy beach if you want Jesus to be Lord of all your life.
    - ❒ There are benefits to making Jesus Lord of your life.
    - ❒ Jesus is into rocks.
    - ❒ Christ wants you to both listen to and obey what he has to say.

13. JESUS IS LORD

THIS WEEK

When young people are asked to confirm and profess their faith in Jesus, they are asked to claim that Jesus is their Lord and Savior. Young people may be clear about what it means to say Jesus is their Savior, but have a harder time understanding the impact of claiming that Jesus is their Lord. It is important to explore what Lordship means and why the early church up through the modern church have recognized Jesus as Lord.

THE OPENER

Begin your discussion time together by asking, **Who is someone in your life you see as an authority figure? In what ways are they someone you listen to when they speak?**

Take time to explore what makes the persons your group members chose authority figures in their lives and in what ways they act as authority figures. Take time to explore why your group members would listen to them and do what they might instruct them to do in their daily lives.

DISCUSSION BY THE NUMBERS (Go through the TalkSheet one item at a time.)

1. Answers will range from "because they are my parents" to "they control my life." The reality is that you choose to make someone an authority figure. It is an act of the will.
2. The answer is, of course, Christ demonstrated that his power extended over nature.
3. After your young people rate the different people on the "Trustworthy Authority Scale" ask, **What makes each authority figure more trustworthy or less trustworthy to you?**
4. Allow the group members to read their completed sentences. Explore with them their responses, always remembering not to judge their answers as right or wrong.
5. Find out which of the answers were chosen most frequently. The point of the activity is to understand that we must listen to and obey Jesus if he is to be Lord over all our lives.

CLOSING DISCUSSION

Christians believe that Jesus' authority comes from God. In **Philippians 2:9-11** Paul quotes a hymn of the early church that reminds us Jesus has authority given to him by God over all life. To say "Jesus Is Lord" is to say we recognize his authority, we choose to listen to him when he speaks, and we have decided to obey him by doing what he asks of us in every area of our lives. Ask, **What makes you want to claim Jesus as YOUR Lord? What makes you want to run away from Jesus as YOUR Lord?**

CLOSING PRAYER

"Dearest Lord Jesus, as your disciple Peter said so long ago, 'To whom shall we go? You have the words of eternal life' (John 6:68). Lord, you alone can calm the wind and tell the waves to be still. You alone can give the blind sight and call the dead to rise. You alone are Lord over all the earth. You alone are Lord of our lives, and we trust your voice and desire to do what you ask of us. Amen."

TalkSheet #14

WHAT DID JESUS DO?

1. A=Agree, D=Disagree. **Read an ancient song of the church about Jesus—Philippians 2:6-11—and then consider the following statements and decide if you agree or disagree. Circle A for agree and D for disagree.**

a. Jesus came to be like God to all of us. A D
b. Jesus was all about making a big splash in history. A D
c. Jesus made a difference in the way people wash their feet. A D
d. Jesus was concerned about what people thought of him. A D
e. Jesus is sitting pretty from now on. A D
f. Jesus has a really cool name. A D

2. Read each of the following Bible passages. Check the one you like the most.

❐ Romans 8:1
❐ 2 Timothy 1:10
❐ 1 Corinthians 8:6
❐ 1 John 5:20
❐ Ephesians 2:6

3. Finish these Sparkplug Sentences:

The thing Jesus did that means the most to me is…

A way Jesus changed my life is…

Something someone told me about Jesus that I will always remember is…

4. Write a favorite thing in the box that you remember Jesus said or did, or a favorite verse about Jesus.

5. African Bible Study – Read Ephesians 2:13-18 three times.

1st Reading – What stands out to you?

2nd Reading – How does this connect with your world?

3rd Reading – What do you feel called to do in response?

14. WHAT DID JESUS DO?

THIS WEEK

Knowing what Jesus did for us is an essential part of the Christian experience. Young people might wonder what this Christian thing is all about. The culture thinks of Jesus as a good teacher, one of history's great religious leaders, or a moralist. But the church remembers Jesus through remembering the cross and resurrection that lifted the curse of sin from humankind and established for us a kingdom where God lives and moves in our lives. Through what Jesus did, God has torn down the barriers that held us apart and has joined us into one family of faith and hope.

THE OPENER

Begin today's discussion by asking, **What is something someone did that made a difference in your life?** Let several volunteers discuss what difference was made and who made it.

DISCUSSION BY THE NUMBERS (Go through the TalkSheet one item at a time.)

1. Use the hymn of the early church, **Philippians 2:6-11**, to talk about what Jesus did.
2. This item gets your youth to look at five different passages that examine what Christ has done for us. See which of the passages were favorites. Ask, **What stands out for you in this passage? What does it tell you about what Jesus did?**
3. Ask the young people to share their completed sentences. Share your responses as well. Completing these sentences should help your group members identify meaningful things about Christ and their lives.
4. Energize your group members' memories of Bible stories about Jesus by sharing a favorite thing you remember that Jesus said or did or your favorite verse about Jesus. Ask, **What makes this your favorite Jesus memory?**
5. Ask your group members to share what stood out to them when they first read Ephesians. Hold off sharing yourself so your group members won't defer to you. Then ask them to share how their second reading connected to their world. And finally, ask what they feel God calling them to do in response to their third reading.

CLOSING DISCUSSION

Christians believe that Jesus came into the world to do something quite amazing: To save us from our sin and establish an everlasting relationship with the Father. He emptied himself, bore witness to the presence and power of God in our lives, showed us what God is like, died on the cross and rose from the dead, went to the Father to prepare a place for us, and ushered in the kingdom of God in our lives and in the world. Christians believe Jesus is God's ultimate and most complete act of love to all humankind. Ask, **Why do you think it is important to remember what Jesus did? What is a question you still have about what Jesus did?**

CLOSING PRAYER

"Dear Lord, you came into the world to save us from sin. You came to establish God's kingdom and get us back into relationship with God our Father. And you accomplished all this by proclaiming the Word, dying for us, rising for us, reigning in power for us. There is so much you did out of love for each and every one of us. Help us, Lord Jesus, to always remember how you went about saving us because of your love for us. Amen."

TalkSheet #15

WHAT IS JESUS DOING RIGHT NOW?

1. **Gimme Five** ways you have represented or might represent your family, school, or church in the world around you.

   1. ______________________________________

   2. ______________________________________

   3. ______________________________________

   4. ______________________________________

   5. ______________________________________

2. **Read John 14:18.** What does Jesus mean when he says, "I will *come to you*"? Choose the most likely answers and tell why.

   a. "You better watch out, you better not cry, you better not pout, I'm telling you why."
   b. There will be a second coming of Jesus.
   c. Jesus comes to us in many ways through friends, family, and others.
   d. It will take him a long time to get from where he is to where we are.
   e. He is promising to encounter us throughout our lives in different ways.

3. Finish these **Sparkplug Sentences:**

   One thing Jesus is doing through my life is…

   To be a part of what Jesus is doing, we need to…

   One thing I notice Jesus doing in the world is…

4. **African Bible Study** – Read **2 Corinthians 5:18-6:1** three times.

   1st Reading – What stands out to you?

   2nd Reading – How does this connect with your world?

   3rd Reading – What do you feel called to do in response?

5. Check off two things from this list of 10 you think you can do to be part of what Jesus is doing now.

   - ☐ Play Rock Band better than anyone else.
   - ☐ Serve in my community at a food bank.
   - ☐ Pass the word on to a school friend about God's love for us in Jesus.
   - ☐ Visit someone in the congregation who is homebound.
   - ☐ Assist in a mentoring program at school.
   - ☐ Get a tattoo that proclaims "Property of Jesus."
   - ☐ Help my family around the house without being asked.
   - ☐ Eat lunch at school with someone considered an "outsider."
   - ☐ Start a Bible fellowship before or after school.
   - ☐ Develop a list of people to pray for every day at school.

15. WHAT IS JESUS DOING RIGHT NOW?

THIS WEEK

Not a person of the past or a mere historical figure, Jesus is very much at work in the world today and active through his Spirit and his church to communicate his message and be his presence. Whenever the body of Christ bears witness to and disperses the Good News of Jesus into the world, it is as his presence to heal a broken world and renew it with the mercy and grace of God.

THE OPENER

Begin this session by asking your young people to talk about a time when they performed an errand for a parent or another person. By performing this errand, they took upon themselves the task of being this person's representative.

When each young person has a situation in mind, explore it, asking, **What were you asked to do and how did you perform your task?** Whether it is going to the store for milk for a parent, mowing the lawn, or delivering something to another, these moments are acts of representation on another's behalf. The discussion leads to how we represent Jesus in the world today by performing "errands" of the gospel.

DISCUSSION BY THE NUMBERS (Go through the TalkSheet one item at a time.)

1. Ask the young people to list five ways they have represented or might represent their family, school, or church in the world around them. Ways young people might represent is through work, shirts with logos, behavior, shared goals, and activities.
2. Ask, **In what ways is your church a way Jesus keeps that promise? How is the Holy Spirit Jesus' answer to that promise?**
3. Listen to your group members' responses. Each of these sentences helps you start a discussion regarding what Jesus is doing right now.
4. This exercise draws your group members deeper into the Scripture and paves the way for a spiritual discipline with Scripture in the future. Explore with them what they learned from reading **2 Corinthians 5:18-6:1** three times. This passage speaks to the fact that God designed the church to work with Christ in bringing about his kingdom on earth.
5. Ask the young people to consider the list provided and to choose two things they could do to be a part of what Jesus is doing now. Discuss how they know this is something Jesus would be doing. Talk about how to make these two things a reality NOW.

CLOSING DISCUSSION

Christians believe that Jesus, the ascended Lord, sits at the right hand of the Father and is at work in the world today through his Spirit and through his body—which is his people, the church. Today it is Jesus proclaiming the Good News into the lives of people and through the lives of people by the power of his Spirit. When we say we are the "priesthood of believers," we mean that as priests we offer the presence of the living Lord to each other and into the world around us. Ask, **In what ways is our church on an errand for Jesus today?**

CLOSING PRAYER

"Dear Lord, thank you for being at work in our lives and in the world. Thanks you for your Spirit and for the church and those who are busy with you in the service of the gospel. Help us listen and be ready to be a part of what you are doing today. Amen."

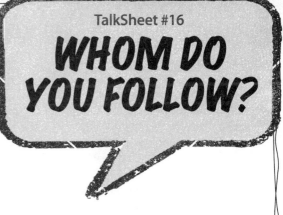

TalkSheet #16

WHOM DO YOU FOLLOW?

1. Rate the following on the "Follow Me" Scale. Rate according to who or what you feel is important to follow by placing the letter of each answer on the scale.

1________2________3________4________5________
No Way! Sometimes

6________7________8________9________10________
I could Here I Come!

a. The current trends in music
b. The opinions of the "popular" kids in school
c. Traffic signs
d. Fashion styles and hairstyle trends
e. Cultural opinions on issues
f. Directions from your teacher

2. Read Matthew 4:18-22. What stands out for you in this reading? Check all that apply.

a. Jesus invites followers.
b. Jesus likes to walk by the sea and watch people fish.
c. In response to Jesus' invitation, they followed "at once" and "immediately."
d. Jesus promises that those who follow him will "fish for men."
e. Following Jesus is in response to his invitation.

3. Finish these Sparkplug Sentences:

To follow Jesus means…

One way I could "drop my nets and follow Jesus" would be to…

With so many voices asking me to follow them every day, it is important for me to…

4. Gimme Five ways you could follow Jesus this next week.

1. ______________________________
2. ______________________________
3. ______________________________
4. ______________________________
5. ______________________________

5. African Bible Study. Read Matthew 6:24 three times and respond following each reading.

1st Reading – What stands out in this text for you?

2nd Reading – How does this text relate to your life right now?

3rd Reading – What do you feel you need to do in response to this text?

16. WHOM DO YOU FOLLOW?

THIS WEEK

We all live in a culture with many voices and invitations to respond with our lives to issues and concerns, fads and fashions. Young people are the target of most of this pressure to follow. It is important to help young people engage the voices and explore what it means to give your life to something or "follow" it in your life. To follow means we give something or someone our time and our energy, making important to us what is important to those we follow. As young people consider what it means to follow Jesus, they must think of how that could take shape in their daily lives.

THE OPENER

We begin this exercise with asking young people to recall a way they have followed someone or something this past week. Since all of us follow someone or something every day, we take time to recognize an act of being a follower and how it took shape in our lives.

Explore with your young people their responses, noting with them how their act of following took shape in their lives. You might comment to them that, **We all follow someone or something every day. In what way were you a follower this past week?**

DISCUSSION BY THE NUMBERS (Go through the TalkSheet one item at a time.)

1. Ask the young people to share their ratings. This item gets your group members talking more about what they follow.
2. Read the Bible text aloud. Then ask your young people to consider the listed responses and decide which one stands out strongest for them from the text and why.
3. Encourage your group members to be as specific as they can about their own life situations as they consider the five ways they can follow Jesus in the next week. Answers like "pray" or "tell others about Jesus" are true but meaningless Sunday school answers. "Pray every morning while I brush my teeth" or "Talk to my friend Rick about what Jesus means to me" are specific and your group members can be held accountable (in the best sense of the word) for doing them.
4. Listen as your group members share their completed sentences. This item takes Jesus out of the Sunday God-building and further into everyday life.
5. Take a moment to explain the African Bible study model to the group. Then read **Matthew 6:24** aloud to them slowly, allowing 30 seconds following each reading before asking the young people to respond to the reading's directives.

CLOSING DISCUSSION

The Christian experience begins when we "drop our nets and follow" Jesus. We live in a culture that asks all of us to follow a variety of voices and issues. To follow means you make what is important to them important to you. Christians believe that when we know who we follow and make a clear decision to be a follower, that has a direct impact on our whole lives. It is important to know who you are following in life. Christians have decided to follow Jesus. Ask, **If you didn't follow Jesus, whom or what would you follow? Why? Why have you decided to follow or not follow Jesus?**

CLOSING PRAYER

"Dear Lord, you come to us and ask us to follow you, not just today or on Sundays, but every day and in every place. There are so many voices in our world asking us to make them important, to do what they say, to follow them. It is hard to know sometimes what to do and who to be. But you say, 'Come, follow me.' Help us know what that means for us as we live each day of our lives. Amen."

TalkSheet #17

IS JESUS THE ONLY WAY?

1. **A=Agree, D=Disagree.** Circle **A** for agree and **D** for disagree.

a. All religions contain some truth in them.	A	D
b. God expresses himself to us as we need to see him.	A	D
c. What matters most about faith is what matters most to you.	A	D
d. Truth is relative according to your perspective.	A	D
e. Jesus Christ IS the only way to a full life.	A	D
f. Faith is believing what you know isn't true.	A	D

2. **Read John 14:5-7.** What is Jesus telling YOU in this reading today about him being the only way? (Check one or more.)

- ❒ Jesus is the way we should live our lives.
- ❒ Jesus IS truth in what he says and does.
- ❒ If we want to see God we better look harder.
- ❒ We now know God personally because of Jesus.
- ❒ Jesus is what life is all about.

3. Finish these **Sparkplug Sentences:**

When I think there is only one way to have a real relationship with God, I think…

If Jesus is the only way, I would need to…

If Jesus were not the only way, it would mean…

One thing that assures me Jesus is the only way is…

4. **Read Romans 9:15.** When it comes to how we practice our faith, why is this statement important to remember? Check three statements most important to how you practice your faith.

- ❒ God is God and you are not.
- ❒ You cannot make God do what you want.
- ❒ God chooses to love us.
- ❒ You always get what you deserve.
- ❒ God's mercy is his to give as he wants.
- ❒ God is totally free to love us as he wants to.
- ❒ Bargaining with God really doesn't work.
- ❒ If you are good, God will like you.
- ❒ We can never deserve God's love.
- ❒ You never can be sure about God's love.

5. **African Bible Study** - Read **Acts 4:8-12** three times and respond following each reading.

1st Reading – What stands out to you?

2nd Reading – How does this connect with your world?

3rd Reading – What do you feel called to do in response?

17. IS JESUS THE ONLY WAY?

THIS WEEK

To many young people our culture presents a varied understanding of God and the many options of faith practices. Young people can be confused about Jesus being the only way and even feel strongly that to make such a claim is judgmental. Our culture teaches young people to see faith and its imperatives as relative, to consider Jesus as an option among the many ways we can choose to understand and relate to God. The Christian faith has historically seen Jesus as the clearest expression of God's presence and God's intention to the world. It is through Jesus alone we are saved.

THE OPENER

Begin by asking the members of your group to consider a game they love to play: **How important to the game are the rules? What would happen if the rules changed with every player? Who establishes the rules for a game?** Usually it is the creator of the game who establishes the rules of how the game is played. So, too, with the "rules" of how we relate to God. Christians believe that it is God himself—and not us—who sets the boundaries on how we relate to him through Jesus.

DISCUSSION BY THE NUMBERS (Go through the TalkSheet one item at a time.)

1. See commentary in bold after each statement:
   - All religions contain some truth. **There may be some truth in every religious belief system but that does not mean they are "the truth" and "the way" to have a right relationship with God.**
   - God expresses himself to us as we need to see him. **No, God expresses himself through Jesus Christ. We can know God through Jesus Christ (see John 1:14-18).**
   - What matters most about faith is what matters most to you. **No way. If this were true then all religions, even ones that contradict each other, would give you a right relationship with God—this doesn't make logical sense, philosophical sense, nor is it biblical.**
   - Truth is relative according to your perspective. **This is what today's secular culture is pushing—no absolutes. This way of thinking (if it is true for you, then it is truth) leads to anarchy. The Bible teaches that Jesus is the way, the truth, and the life (John 14:6).**
   - Jesus Christ IS the only way to a full life. **The apostle Peter tells us that only Jesus has the words of life (John 6:68). Jesus said he came to give us a full life (see John 10:10).**
   - Faith is believing what you know isn't true. **There are those who believe this. The reality—faith is putting your trust in someone or something you know you can rely on. Jesus has shown us through Scripture and through our life experiences that we can rely on him.**
2. Ask your young people to listen as you read the Bible text aloud, then have them talk about which of the following statements represents what stands out for them most from this reading.
3. Listen to your group members' completed sentences and start a conversation about Jesus being the one and only Way.
4. Ask your group to listen as you read aloud **Romans 9:15** slowly twice. Then ask, **When it comes to how we practice our faith, which three of these statements expresses what is most important for you to remember from this Bible reading?**
5. Using the African Bible study method, read the text slowly and clearly three times, asking your young people to respond after each reading to the reflection question. (Note: This text from Acts highlights Peter's strong statement of belief in the supremacy of Jesus Christ as the only means by which God acts to save humanity. Peter proclaims Jesus as crucified and as resurrected from the dead. God has made Jesus the foundational stone upon which God's mercy is expressed to all mankind.)

CLOSING DISCUSSION

Christians believe that God has established this relationship with us. It is God's making and not something we have fashioned. God is free to set the guidelines for how this relationship works and how it does not work. Christians believe that though we can develop all kinds of notions about God and how we should relate to God, it is God himself who has expressed through Jesus how he works in our lives and how we are to respond. The Christian experience is based upon the notion that Christianity is a relationship established by God himself. Say, **Jesus clearly tells us that he is *the* Way, *the* Truth, and *the* Life. Ask, Do you believe this? Why or why not?** Ask, **Why is seeing Jesus as the way through which we have a relationship with God important in the Christian experience?**

CLOSING PRAYER

"Dear Father, left to ourselves we could come up with all kinds of ways to see you and think we know you. But we thank you that you have not left us to figure it out our way, but that you have come to us and have communicated to us through Jesus your intent, your hope, and your way to really knowing you. Amen."

SECTION 4 QUESTIONS ABOUT THE HOLY SPIRIT

But the Helper, the Holy Spirit, whom the Father will send in My name, He will teach you all things, and bring to your remembrance all that I said to you. **(John 14:26 NASB)**

Introduce the Topic

Allow Enough Time

AFFIRM ALL RESPONSES—RIGHT OR WRONG

Don't Be the Authoritative Answer

LISTEN TO EACH PERSON

Don't Force It

Don't Take Sides

LET THEM LAUGH!

Allow Silence

BE CREATIVE AND FLEXIBLE

Be There for Your Kids

TalkSheet #18

THE HOLY SPIRIT

1. GIMME FIVE – List five things you can "see" God doing in your world.

1. ______________________________

2. ______________________________

3. ______________________________

4. ______________________________

5. ______________________________

2. Read John 14:15-18. What is the most important thing you wish to remember from this reading?

- ❒ The Holy Spirit is really spooky.
- ❒ The Holy Spirit of God is a powerful presence in believer's lives.
- ❒ The world will have trouble with believing in the Holy Spirit.
- ❒ God's Holy Spirit is with us every day.
- ❒ Jesus will not leave us alone but will be coming to us wherever we are.
- ❒ The Holy Spirit is God's companionship with us.
- ❒ Truth is what the Holy Spirit will bring to us.

3. Yes-No-Maybe So. Consider the following statements and determine if they are actions of the Holy Spirit. (Y=Yes, N=No, MB=Maybe So.) The Holy Spirit—

_____ stops me from doing stupid things.
_____ makes me look better than I would usually look.
_____ helps me read the minds of others.
_____ gives me insights into the Bible I would never have seen.
_____ gives me an awareness of my own need for Jesus.
_____ gives me the winning lottery number.
_____ prompts me to avoid temptation.
_____ lets me know God's will in a situation.
_____ finds a parking place for me when the mall is crowded.
_____ gives me answers to math homework.

4. Finish these Sparkplug Sentences:

One way I think the Holy Spirit is important in my life is…

A neat thing about the Holy Spirit is…

Knowing God's Spirit is in my life makes me want to…

5. African Bible Study – Read Galatians 5:22-25 three times and respond following each reading.

1st Reading – What stands out to you?

2nd Reading – How does this connect with your world?

3rd Reading – What do you feel called to do in response?

THIS WEEK

Understanding the Holy Spirit's presence in our lives is something young people often have misconceptions about. From the first moments in creation, the Holy Spirit has moved across the face of the waters and in the lives of God's people. It was God's promise to pour out his Spirit into the lives of his people, and beginning with Pentecost the Spirit has moved to create out of people from all over the world a family of faith and hope: the church. It is important to explore with young people how the Holy Spirit is a vital part of the Christian understanding or the work and presence of God.

THE OPENER

Begin this session with an exercise that invites the young people to consider an image from life that is also an image from Scripture. In the first five books of the Bible, the Pentateuch, the Hebrew word for "breath"—*Ruach* (Roo-ahch), or *spirit*—expresses the invisible movement or creative activity of God, powerful and pervasive, like wind across the surface of the water. As our breath is strength and power to us, so, too, is the Spirit to God.

Read Genesis 1:1-2 to your young people and then explore this image with them. Ask, Have you ever noticed wind moving the surface of water or moving leaves? How is this image a good expression of the Spirit of God in your life?

DISCUSSION BY THE NUMBERS (Go through the TalkSheet one item at a time.)

1. Remember seeing God's movement is LIKE seeing the water moving as the wind passes over it. We see the water move and know it is the wind even though we can't see it. Listen to your young people's lists of five and include your own five in the discussion.
2. Read the Bible text from the Gospel of John and ask your young people to talk about which two statements best reflect what they believe is most important for them to remember from this reading.
3. See commentary in bold after each statement:
   The Holy Spirit—
   - gives me insights into the Bible I would never have seen. **Yes, the Holy Spirit illuminates God's Word for us.**
   - stops me from doing stupid things. **No. You have free will and get to choose to do smart or stupid things.**
   - gives me the winning lottery number. **No way! And aren't you too young to be playing the lottery?**
   - makes me look better than I would usually look. **You get to be in charge of your own appearance.**
   - prompts me to avoid temptation. **Yes, the Holy Spirit is like this holy teleprompter (as the Newsboys say) that nudges you to run or resist temptation.**
   - finds a parking place for me when the mall is crowded. **Can't you find your own parking space?**
   - helps me read the minds of others. **Mind your own business, much?**
   - gives me an awareness of my own need for Jesus. **Yes!**
   - lets me know God's will in a situation. **Yes, but we must learn to listen. Cultivating an ear that listens to the Holy Spirit takes spiritual discipline.**
   - gives me answers to math homework. **No, that requires hard work called *studying*.**
4. Listen to the completed sentences. This will help you get a faith conversation going about the Holy Spirit in the lives of your group members.
5. **African Bible studies** are fun because each of your group members will have interesting perspectives on the passage. Listen to see how the Holy Spirit used **Galatians 5:22-25** in the lives of your group members.

CLOSING DISCUSSION

Christians believe that God's Holy Spirit moves within the world and in our lives. The Holy Spirit is an essential presence in our lives who enlivens our lives to God's saving Word, moving within us to transform our lives into the image of God's Son, Jesus. The presence of the Holy Spirit in our lives produces certain characteristics that are an important part of the Christian experience. Read **1 Corinthians 3:16** and ask, **How is the Holy Spirit of God in your life an essential key to your Christian experience? What is most confusing about the Holy Spirit? Most exciting? Most difficult to believe?**

CLOSING PRAYER

"Dear Holy Spirit, thank you that you live and move in our lives with your living presence. Amen."

TalkSheet #19

WE ARE THE BODY OF CHRIST

1. Consider **your family** and how different members might provide something that in some way helps the whole family? (Who shops, cooks, mows, cleans, writes checks…?)

2. How committed are you to being part of your congregation?

   - ❒ Totally committed
   - ❒ Committed most days
   - ❒ Committed some days
   - ❒ Not very committed
   - ❒ Not committed at all

3. Read **1 Corinthians 12:12-27.** How is the church like Jesus' body in the world?

   - ❒ It is sometimes very messy.
   - ❒ Each part is nothing without all the other parts.
   - ❒ You cannot treat your eye like you do your foot.
   - ❒ God created each of us unique and special.
   - ❒ Each of us has special skills others need.
   - ❒ Christians should bathe more often.
   - ❒ We need to really work together to get anywhere.

4. Finish these **Sparkplug Sentences:**

   When I think about being in Jesus' body it makes me…

   As a body, we need to…

   To be in Jesus' body is like…

5. **IN the Body!** Where are you? (Consider where you fit in the "body" and why you are that body part.)

19. WE ARE THE BODY OF CHRIST

THIS WEEK

In our culture we tend to think and act as if we are independent of each other and that our actions do not have a lasting effect on the whole gathering. We speak of our independence and say, "As long as I don't hurt anyone it doesn't matter what I do." But the Bible teaches us that we ARE connected and that we are in fact like a body. Young people need to hear the voice of the Christian community about interconnectedness and what it means to be the body of Christ together.

THE OPENER

Begin by asking your group members to consider their own bodies and how each part provides for the whole. Ask, **How does the elbow contribute to the rest of your body? How about your big toe?**

Be aware they may feel awkward speaking about their bodies and that it might be easy to joke about the topic. This is fine. The point will be made as you follow up with the questions that the body has many specified parts that do provide important functions for the well-being of the whole. Trust Paul's image to help your young people think about their relationship with each other.

DISCUSSION BY THE NUMBERS (Go through the TalkSheet one item at a time.)

1. Family is another metaphor to get your group talking about the different roles/functions people, including them, play in the church.
2. This item gets specific about the commitment level of your group members to your congregation. Don't go for the Sunday school answer. Ask your group for a seriously honest answer.
3. Read the Bible text aloud and then ask the young people to consider the statements and talk about the two that best reflect what the text is saying to them.
4. Listen to your group members' completed sentences and get a faith conversation going about being a body part in Jesus' body. Talk about how everyone in the group who is in Christ is a body part—whether healthy and functioning properly or sickly and falling apart.
5. Help your group members imagine the outline of a body in your meeting room with a head and face, arms and hands, torso, legs and feet, etc. Ask the young people to consider where they think they are presently in the body and why. Then have them stand at that place in the body. Allow time for each young person to share where they are and why.

CLOSING DISCUSSION

Christians believe that together we are the body of Christ in the world and that as individuals wherever we are we still play a part in the whole expression of Jesus to the world. The body is made up of people of different ages, races, genders, classes, skills, and attitudes. Whether globally, locally, in a small group, or with one other person—we each play our part. Listen to **Ephesians 4:16**. Each of us, as we do our part in the body, makes the whole body stronger in love and purpose. Ask, **What part do we play in each other's growth as a Christian?**

CLOSING PRAYER

"Dear Father, you have given us forgiveness, you have given us grace, and you have given us one another. Sometimes we forget we play an important part in each other's lives and in the life of the whole church. You remind us we are your fingers and your voice in the world. Help us to find our place in your body that the whole body might grow in love. Amen."

TalkSheet #20

COMMUNION

The Feast of Belonging

1. A=Agree, D=Disagree. Circle A for agree and D for disagree.

a. People who wear similar clothes usually belong together.	A	D
b. Common interests make people feel comfortable with each other.	A	D
c. Music interests are a clear way people find where they belong.	A	D
d. Attending the same school helps people to belong.	A	D
e. Having the same beliefs is essential for people to belong together.	A	D

2. Read Matthew 26:26-30. In what ways do you think Jesus takes the bread and cup and makes them a feast for belonging? (Pick two.)

- ❒ Jesus tells us he is giving himself to each of us.
- ❒ A simple meal becomes a witness of God's love for us.
- ❒ Yuck—is that cup really filled with blood?
- ❒ There is no better way for Jesus to express the fullness of his commitment to us.
- ❒ We all share together Jesus' gift of himself.
- ❒ Jesus has changed every meal into a time to remember him.

3. Finish these Sparkplug Sentences:

To feel like I belong I need to experience…

One way I experience community is…

When I take Communion with my congregation I…

4. Gimme Five ways Paul's words in 2 Corinthians 5:14-18 express belonging to you.

1. ______________________________

2. ______________________________

3. ______________________________

4. ______________________________

5. ______________________________

5. Read 1 Corinthians 11:26. What does this passage have to do with Communion?

- ❒ Every meal is a time to remember Jesus.
- ❒ Only a certain kind of bread and particular cup should be used.
- ❒ We remember together that he is coming again.
- ❒ When we remember this together we are proclaiming Jesus' promise.
- ❒ We remember Jesus' body was broken and his blood poured out for us.
- ❒ We are reminded that doing this together really matters.

20. COMMUNION: The Feast of Belonging

THIS WEEK

Belonging is a big issue for young people. So much energy is spent on fitting in to whatever norm they desire to associate with in school and in the culture. The pressure to "fit in" is a big part of the peer pressure young people experience. The church offers wonderful GOOD NEWS expressed through the celebration of communion, the sharing of the common bread broken and cup poured in Christ's name. It literally can be seen as a Feast of Belonging.

THE OPENER

Begin by asking your young people to consider and discuss what "belonging" means to them. It is a good way to explore with them how belonging is expressed, experienced, shared, seen, and understood. Begin by asking, **What does it mean to you to "belong"?**

Then when you feel the group is ready, explore with them how they understand belonging. You might end this exercise by asking, **How important is it for someone to know they belong?**

DISCUSSION BY THE NUMBERS (Go through the TalkSheet one item at a time.)

1. See commentary in bold after each statement.
   - People who wear similar clothes usually belong together. **In most cases these people are within the same clique or social grouping at school.**
   - Common interests make people feel comfortable with each other. **Often they do. People who love chemistry enjoy talking about chemistry. And people who are competitive swimmers talk swimming.**
   - Music interests are a clear way people find where they belong. **Today's youth culture is often fragmented into groupings by musical taste.**
   - Attending the same school helps people to belong. **This can be true but the bigger the school, the less connected to each other students will be.**
   - Having the same beliefs is essential for people to belong together. **Members of a congregation tend to share common core beliefs and act together on those beliefs.**
2. Read the text aloud and ask your young people to consider the provided statements and discuss the two that best represent for them what is important to remember from the text.
3. Ask the young people to complete the incomplete sentences. These **Sparkplug Sentences** are designed to create conversation in your group. Avoid trying to correct their responses. Allow them to safely express themselves with these sentences.
4. After reading this Bible text together, ask your young people to talk about five aspects of belonging expressed in this reading. Note: Some aspects could be all sharing in Jesus' death, sharing a new way we look at each other, each of us being reconciled to God.
5. Read the Bible text and ask your young people to discuss the statements that best captures what stands out for them from the reading.

CLOSING DISCUSSION

Christians believe that because of Jesus we belong to a new family of God. Through the act of giving himself for us—his body broken on the cross and his blood "poured" forth in the crucifixion—we are brought into a new reality of belonging. Through the celebration of common bread "broken" for us and a common cup "poured" for us, we celebrate this new community with one another in God's presence through the power of God's Holy Spirit. In communion we remember who we are and whose we are because of Jesus Christ. In Christ we belong. Ask, **If communion is an important expression of the church of Jesus Christ, then how important do you think it is to Christ that we know we belong? Do you feel like you belong? Why or why not?**

CLOSING PRAYER

"Dear Lord, you have expressed your love for us on the cross. With a simple loaf of bread broken and shared, and a simple cup poured and shared, you ask us to remember you. And in remembering you we can't help but remember who we are because of you. Thank you, Lord, for the celebration of communion to remind us we belong to you and with each other. Amen."

TalkSheet #21

WHAT'S THIS ABOUT BAPTISM?

1. **Involved/Committed.** **Consider the following and determine who is involved and who is committed:**

    a. A punk rocker shaves his head to attend a concert.
    Involved *Committed*
    b. A Marine wears a uniform.
    Involved *Committed*
    c. A marching band member attends a game.
    Involved *Committed*
    d. A football player cheers teammates from the bench.
    Involved *Committed*
    e. A young man attending a dance sits at a table.
    Involved *Committed*
    f. A young person attends class but does not do homework.
    Involved *Committed*
    g. A young bride says "I do" at her wedding.
    Involved *Committed*

2. **Read Acts 2:37-42. When people asked Peter what they should do in response to Jesus, what did he tell them and what happened next?**

3. **PIT STOP: Baptism means "dipping or plunging into water." In what ways do you think water is a good image for a changed life?**

    - ❒ You fish in water.
    - ❒ Water is a great cleaning agent.
    - ❒ You can drown in water.
    - ❒ When you come up for air after diving into a pool you feel refreshed.
    - ❒ Being near water is relaxing.
    - ❒ A flood changes your life.
    - ❒ Water splashed on your face will wake you up.
    - ❒ Water puts out a house fire.

4. **Finish these Sparkplug Sentences:**

    The last time I watched a baptism I thought…

    What I like most about baptism is…

    What I wonder about baptism is…

5. **Baptism implies that the one baptized dedicates her total life to the triune God—the Father, the Son, and the Holy Spirit—that through Christ's death and resurrection she is saved from her sins and has a solid hope of eternal life. What do you think it means to live out your baptism? How seriously do you live out your baptism?**

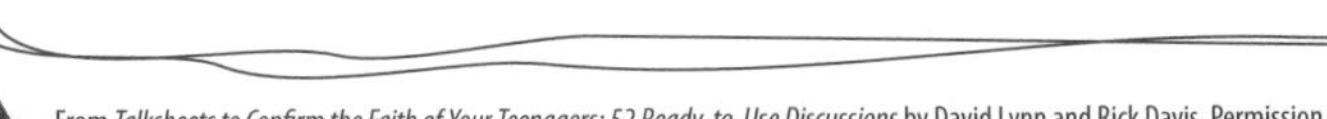

21. WHAT'S THIS ABOUT BAPTISM?

THIS WEEK

Baptism is an important sacrament of the Christian community. While many young people may have the opportunity to watch a baptism, they often have confused notions concerning the rite. This session is designed to open up discussion and provide an opportunity for young people to encounter and discuss some key texts concerning baptism.

THE OPENER

Begin by asking your young people to consider expressions of belonging and participation they encounter every day in the culture around them—classrooms, teams, cliques. We all express our desire to belong and "fit in" through styles, behaviors, and attitudes. As people of faith, we express our sense of the community we belong to and identify with through expressions of faith. Baptism is one act of obedience all Christians do once to express our belonging in Jesus as our Lord and Savior.

Explore ways people express a desire to belong or participate with a group or clique. Then ask, **In what ways do we express our desire to belong and participate with each other in a common faith in Jesus Christ?**

DISCUSSION BY THE NUMBERS (Go through the TalkSheet one item at a time.)

1. Ask the young people to consider the eight people listed and determine whether they think they are only "Involved" or if they are "Committed."
2. A reading of **Acts 2:37-42** shows that the people, once they were given the facts about Jesus, were amazed, turned their lives over to God (an inward change) as evidenced by the symbolic gesture of baptism (an outward sign of the inward change). Baptism was seen as important, not because it saved the people, but as a symbol that represented salvation.
3. Here you are asking your young people to consider the physical act of baptism and how it is a good image in the life of the church for a changed life. If possible, have a bowl of water with you and with your hands lift and drop the water, creating a splashing sound. Ask the young people to consider the water and its spiritual image in the life of the church. Ask, **What makes water a good image of a new life in Christ?**

❒ You fish in water.
❒ Water is a great cleaning agent.
❒ You can drown in water.
❒ When you come up for air after diving into a pool you feel refreshed.
❒ Being near water is relaxing.
❒ A flood changes your life.
❒ Water splashed on your face will wake you up.
❒ Water puts out a house fire.

4. Listen to your group members' responses. Take this time to answer any questions they may have about baptism. This is your chance to talk about your congregation's distinctive beliefs about baptism.
5. Get everyone's perspective on what it means to live out one's baptism—everything from a dedicated involvement in the body of Christ (the church) to service in Christ's name. Find out how many in your group are serious about living out their baptism.

CLOSING DISCUSSION

Christians believe that Jesus gave us an example **(Matthew 3:13-15)** and a command **(Matthew 28:19-20)** demonstrating the importance of this rite of belonging. We believe that in baptism people repent and believe in Jesus as their Lord and Savior, they are baptized with water in the name of the Father and the Son and the Holy Spirit, they receive the promise of the Holy Spirit, and they belong to the body of believers all over the world. Ask, **Why do you think baptism is important in our relationship with Jesus?**

CLOSING PRAYER

"Dear Father, you promised to cleanse us from within and to fill us with your Spirit, and you have given us each other to walk with and to learn from. By the act of baptism given in your name, we realize we offer ourselves to your cleansing touch and healing presence, and take our place in the community of faith. Thank you for this image of hope and life called baptism. Amen."

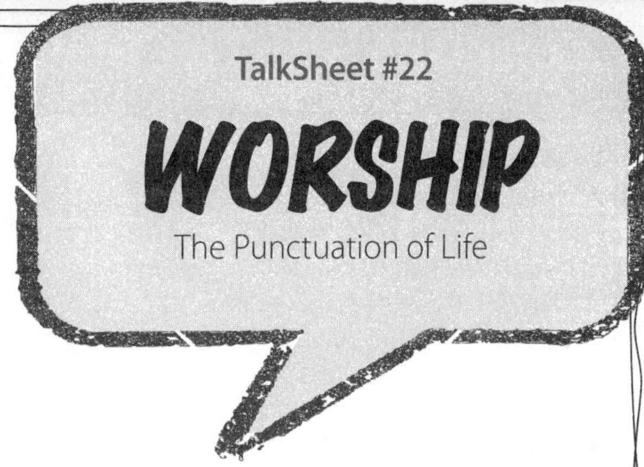

1. Read and consider the following:

Just before she laughed out loud and he said oh come on I laughed and yet she did not stop now he was mad I want to know something to keep him from shouting she kept silent

What is missing here and what difference does that make?

2. Rate your week on the "My Week's Big 8" Scale: List at least 8 things you "must" do every week and rate them by placing the letter on the scale.

I_______2_______3_______4_______5_______6_______7_______8_______9_______10_______
Not important — Kinda important — Important — Essential

a.
b.
c.
d.
e.
f.
g.
h.

3. Read Hebrews 10:24-25. Why do you think worshiping with others is a good habit?

- ❒ It gets you out of the house on the weekends.
- ❒ We get to encourage each other weekly in our faith.
- ❒ You become part of a community of other believers.
- ❒ Being with God becomes an important part of every week.
- ❒ Good habits take time to build.
- ❒ What else can you do on Sunday morning?
- ❒ It sets a mood for the rest of the week.
- ❒ Other

4. Read this short story:

A man was driving his family to church on a very rainy Sunday morning, considering that he might just turn around and drive home, when he saw someone he knew from church walking with an umbrella on the side of the road. He pulled over and offered the man a ride. "Thanks," said the man. "I don't have a car to drive so thanks for the lift."

"Why would you decide to go to church on a rainy day like this?" asked the driver.

"Oh, today's rain isn't a part of my decision. I decided to go to church today many years ago," said the man.

What does this story tell us of worship and the rhythm of life?

5. Rate from least true to most true. Place a number from 1 through 5 on the lines below, with 1 being the least true and 5 being the most true.

_____ Corporate worship (worship with others) in my congregation helps me work better during the week.
_____ People are made to take a rest day once a week.
_____ The Sabbath is a good time to get extra tasks done I usually can't finish.
_____ A Sabbath day helps me remember who I am.
_____The Sabbath is a friendly revolt against the pressures of life.

22. WORSHIP: The Punctuation of Life

THIS WEEK

Worship is an essential rhythm of the Christian experience. You could say worship is the punctuation of life. This week we consider worship as the key punctuation to our life's "sentence" that expresses in us purpose, perspective, and meaning. It's important to shepherd young people in understanding the importance of worship in the rhythm of their week. This week we ask the young people to consider how they spend their weeks and what is their week's punctuation or expression of meaning. Discovering the importance of weekly worship is an important part of faithful living in response to God.

THE OPENER

Begin by asking your group this question: **What is the first word that comes to mind when you hear the word *worship*?**

DISCUSSION BY THE NUMBERS (Go through the TalkSheet one item at a time.)

1. Punctuation adds essential pauses, emphasis, highlights, and direction to each gathering of words. Without punctuation, a collection of words does not make sense. The same can be true for the activities of a week. With young people crowding activities into their daily lives, so often the meaning of life can be evasive. How might punctuation help us understand the words and what they mean? Do you think our weeks have punctuation in them that also helps with understanding and meaning?
2. Listen for how your group members rated the eight essential activities. Talk about the need for punctuation in the middle of these activities.
3. Ask your young people to listen to the Bible text and then consider the offered statements. Ask them to choose two (or write another statement or two) that best represent for them why worshiping weekly is a good habit. When all have shared, talk about how worship is punctuation to the week.
4. The man decided to go to church weekly. The rain was an event of the day. Worship is an event established years ago in the man's life as a weekly rhythm. The man worshiped with other Christians as a habit in his week. Ask your young people how this story expresses this man's punctuation in his week.
5. Ask the young people to consider the following and rate them from truer to less true and then explore these with the young people.

CLOSING DISCUSSION

Christians believe that worship is an important part of our weekly rhythm of life. It is a way of seeing the world in the light of God. Worship reminds us of our relationship with God and grounds us in a healthy perspective of life and faith. Weekly worship sets the tone for living faithfully in this world. Ask, **Why do you think weekly worship can establish a strong, clear "punctuation" in someone's life?**

CLOSING PRAYER

"Dear Father, we thank you for the gift of worship. Thank you for time to stop and remember you in our lives, to celebrate our relationship, and to spend time with brothers and sisters in faith. Teach us to consider the rhythm of our weeks, to celebrate our hope, and to remember you in our lives. Father, let worship punctuate our lives with faith. Amen."

TalkSheet #23

R U GIFTED?

1. Rate the following on the "Important Skills" Scale by placing each letter on the scale.

1________2________3________4________5________
None Some

6________7________8________9________10________
Good Better Best

a. Ability to play computer games quite well.
b. Ability to tutor another in math or English.
c. Ability to communicate in another language.
d. Ability to play music well (radio doesn't count).
e. Ability to lead a group in the outdoors safely.
f. Ability to play a sport with great success.

2. Read 1 Corinthians 12:4-7. Decide which statements are True (T) and which are False (F).

___ God gave you whatever interests, talents, skills, or abilities you have.
___ One's gifts should be used to get ahead in life.
___ Some people have more than one gift that can be used to serve others.
___ Only Christians are given gifts that can be used to serve others.
___ A person who doesn't use his gifts for God is wasting them.

3. Most people in our congregation use their special gift or gifts to serve others. (Check one.)

- ❒ I strongly agree
- ❒ I agree.
- ❒ I disagree.
- ❒ I strongly disagree.
- ❒ I don't care.

4. Finish these Sparkplug Sentences:

My gifts are important to me because…

My gifts are important to others in that…

I hope that with the gifts God has given me I might…

5. African Bible Study – Read Ephesians 4:11-12 three times and respond following each reading.

1st Reading – What stands out to you?

2nd Reading – How does this connect with your world?

3rd Reading – What do you feel called to do in response?

23. R U GIFTED?

THIS WEEK

Everyone has an ability to do something, but we too often recognize the more visible abilities and give them greater honor and ignore the more subtle abilities that are still essential to each of us. Young people can often feel they do not have abilities if they are not highly praised in school. It is important to see that each one has something to offer and that these abilities are "gifted" by God to us not simply for our own enjoyment but for the common good. Everyone has a place in God's kingdom that can be filled only by that person.

THE OPENER

Ask, **What skills are needed to watch television?** This will get your group members thinking about skills, abilities, talents, and gifts.

DISCUSSION BY THE NUMBERS (Go through the TalkSheet one item at a time.)

1. The ratings will get your group members debating the relative importance of the six abilities listed. All can be used to serve God.
2. See commentary in bold after each statement.
   - Whatever interests, talents, skills, or abilities you have were given to you by God. **Everything we have is provided for us by God whether or not we believe in God's existence.**
   - One's gifts should be used to get ahead in life. **This is most often how people see it rather than seeing one's gifts as a God-given way to serve others.**
   - Some people have more than one gift that can be used to serve others. **Most of us have multiple skills, talents, abilities, and gifts.**
   - Only Christians are given gifts that can be used to serve others. **Everyone has ways they can serve others. It can be argued that Holy Spirit-influenced gifts are uniquely given to Christians to serve others through the church. Others would argue that everyone is given at least one gift, whether a believer in Christ or not, to be used to serve others because God cares about the common good.**
   - A person who doesn't use their gifts for God is wasting them. **Yes, and it's sad when they are wasted in selfish ways.**
3. See if there is agreement. Then get a faith conversation going about your congregation's people. Use the discussion as a time to talk about how your young people can role model using their spiritual gifts to serve the congregation and the world.
4. Oftentimes, young people will get hung up about identifying their particular God-given gift. Don't go there. Ask your young people to do a quick survey of what they are good at and how these abilities, gifts, talents, or skills can best serve others. It is too easy to get caught up in the identification of gifts such that they never get used within the church.
5. Remind the young people how to do an **African Bible** study. This exercise draws your group members deeper into the Scripture as you talk about **Ephesians 4:11-12.**

CLOSING DISCUSSION

Christians believe that each of us is created on purpose and with intention by God. That means we each have a place in the world and in the body of Christ that only we can fill. Each of us has particular interests and abilities that demonstrate themselves in our daily lives. Some are good at athletics, some at learning, some at music, some are better listeners while others are better speakers, and many, many more. The Christian experience reminds us to consider our gifts and the gifts of others as God-given for the common good. Ask, **Why is understanding that each of us has a gift for the common good important in the Christian experience?**

CLOSING PRAYER

"Dear Father, so often we just don't see the bigger picture of how all our gifts are needed, and how all our gifts might benefit each other. Help us, Father, to appreciate not only our gifts and interests, abilities and skills, but also those of others. Help us know that you have created a bigger picture in which we all have an important role. Amen."

SECTION 5 QUESTIONS ABOUT THE BIBLE

I have hidden your word in my heart that I might not sin against you. **(Psalm 119:11)**

AFFIRM ALL RESPONSES—RIGHT OR WRONG

Don't Be the Authoritative Answer

LISTEN TO EACH PERSON

Don't Force It

Don't Take Sides

LET THEM LAUGH!

Allow Silence

BE CREATIVE AND FLEXIBLE

Be There for Your Kids

TalkSheet #24

THE NEXT VOICE YOU HEAR

1. Consider the following "messages." Place the letter of each message on the line scale according to the influence it might have upon your life.

1________2________3________4________5________
Least influence

6________7________8________9________10________
Most influence

a. An assignment on the blackboard from your teacher.
b. A note found in the hallway at your school.
c. A request from your dad or mom about a chore that needs doing.
d. A severe weather warning in the corner of your TV screen.
e. A pink slip from the principal asking you to come to the office.

2. What gives some voices more influence or authority in our lives over others? (Choose your top ONE.)

a. If the voice is good looking and of the opposite sex, it has influence on my life.
b. If the voice can hurt me, it has influence on my life.
c. If the voice gets me money, it has influence on my life.
d. If the voice influences my future, it has influence on my life.
e. If the voice promotes my well-being, it has influence on my life.

3. Finish these Sparkplug Sentences:

For a voice to have authority in my life, it needs to…

Something said to me once that I will never forget is…

The Bible as "God's Word" means that…

4. A=Agree, D=Disagree. Circle A for agree and D for disagree.

a. When it comes to how I live my life, the Bible doesn't have much to say to me.	A	D
b. The Bible is mostly for old people who want to get into heaven.	A	D
c. What I do when I am alone is my own business, no one else's.	A	D
d. The Bible is filled with nice stories, most of them not true.	A	D
e. I want to live my life based upon what the Bible says.	A	D

5. How true is Psalm 119:105 in your life?

- ❒ I have no clue what it means.
- ❒ The Bible is a guide for every decision I make.
- ❒ The Bible is a guide for most of the decisions I make.
- ❒ The Bible is a guide for some of the decisions I make.
- ❒ I don't use the Bible to guide my life.

Your word is a lamp to my feet and a light for my path. ***(Psalm 119:105)***

24. THE NEXT VOICE YOU HEAR

THIS WEEK
A big issue for young people in America today is authority. With all the voices young people hear each day, whom should they really listen to above all others? Which voices ought to have more weight and why? How do they choose to listen and give weight to a voice in their lives? This week's focus is on Scripture as the voice of importance in their lives. With so many voices out there claiming so many truths and offering so many opinions, it is important for young Christians to come to terms with the notion of the authority of Scripture over their lives.

THE OPENER
Ask the following two questions to get your group members talking about the influence of different voices in their lives: **How often do you listen to music? How much influence does your music have on your life?**

DISCUSSION BY THE NUMBERS (Go through the TalkSheet one item at a time.)

1. The purpose of this activity is to explore how we select different "voices" in our lives as having more value than other voices and therefore greater influence. Take time to see how your group members placed their values, giving each young person time to discuss why they placed one "voice" above another in influence. Young people may have their own different reasons for valuing a "voice" at this time in their lives or in a particular situation.

2. See which was the most common choice of your group members and why. Then challenge your group to talk about different ways to describe *authority* without using the word *authority*. Here's a definition of *authority* that may help guide your dialogue:

   Authority: the power to persuade or influence that is the result of expertise, knowledge, experience, position, or force.

3. Listen to the completed sentences. Point out that everyone has voices of authority in his life, whether it is the Bible, a parent, an employer, a girlfriend, a boyfriend, or others.
4. These Agree/Disagree statements get a discussion going about who is in charge of the lives of your group members. Ask, **Are you in charge of your life or is God through his written Word, the Bible, in charge?**
5. Christians see the Bible as having authority to speak about God, salvation, faith, relationships, and life. Go back to the first exercise and ask your group members to decide where they would put Scripture (indicated by the letter S) on the continuum. Take a moment as a leader to share how and why you give weight to Scripture in your life as a voice to listen to above other voices.

CLOSING DISCUSSION
Christians see the Bible as the voice of truth. We believe the Bible has authority because it's the written Word of God. This is why we take reading it and learning it so seriously. It's a word that matters. Ask your group, **Why should the Bible have authority over the lives of Christians?**

CLOSING PRAYER
"Dear Father, we thank you for your written Word. Help us understand the true value of Scripture in our lives as a word we can trust and as a word we can count on to offer us a true and honest perspective about what really matters in life. In your dear son Jesus' name we pray. Amen."

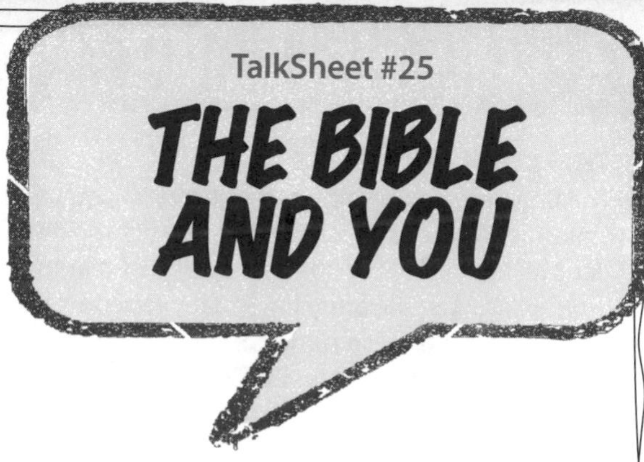

1. **A=Agree, D=Disagree. Circle A for agree and D for disagree.**

a. The Bible offers answers to all life's problems.	A	D
b. The Bible should be taken literally.	A	D
c. The Bible is not often easy to understand.	A	D
d. The Bible does not answer every question.	A	D
e. The Bible has many writers but one point.	A	D
f. The Bible means different things to different people.	A	D

2. **Read Psalm 119:9-11.** In what ways does this psalm speak for you? In what ways does this psalm challenge you?

3. **ADD-ON.** Add your own line to **Psalm 119:11.**

Psalm 119:11.2 ____

4. **Finish these Sparkplug Sentences:**

I think I could get into the Bible if…

The most difficult thing about reading the Bible is…

The neatest thing about the Bible to me is…

5. **African Bible Study** – Read **2 Timothy 3:16-17** three times and respond following each reading.

1st Reading – What stands out to you?

2nd Reading – How does this connect with your world?

3rd Reading – What do you feel called to do in response?

25. THE BIBLE AND YOU

THIS WEEK
The Bible is an important part of every Christian's discipleship. At the same time we know that most Christians have not developed a good habit of reading the Bible. Young people often have many misconceptions about the Bible. It is important for young people to understand how valuable the Bible is to our Christian experience for faith and understanding.

THE OPENER
Begin by asking the members of your group to share a Bible story or verse(s) they remember and consider their favorite. Allow a few moments for each member of your group to choose at least one thing they remember from the Bible.

DISCUSSION BY THE NUMBERS (Go through the TalkSheet one item at a time.)
1. Ask the young people to consider the statements and determine if they agree or disagree with each. Have those who agree move to one side of your meeting area and those who disagree move to the other side. Explore with your group the reasoning behind their responses.
2. Listen to your group members' responses to the questions based upon **Psalm 119:9-11**.
3. This activity is not trying to get your young people to add to the Bible. Rather, it is attempting to get them to expand their understanding of the Bible. Ask volunteers to read their **Psalm 119:11.2**. Then ask someone to read **Psalm 119:9 through 119:11.2** out loud.
4. Listen to the completed sentences. Questions will arise about the Bible you can explore with your group.
5. Remind the young people how to do an African Bible study. Let different group members share their insights into **2 Timothy 3:16-17**.

CLOSING DISCUSSION
Christians believe the Bible is important in our Christian experience and understanding. While many different voices speak through the stories, poems, recorded events, proclamations, and letters in the Bible, we believe it is one Voice that has spoken and is speaking through these writings to us. God has given us the gift of this written Word to make himself known to us as we read and listen to the Bible in our daily lives. Ask, **Why do you think the Bible is important to us if we are going to be a part of the Christian experience?** Then ask, **When was the last time the Bible spoke to you?**

CLOSING PRAYER
"Dear Father, thank you for the written Word that helps us to know you, to know what it means to walk with you in a relationship, and to know how wonderfully you have reached out to us in Jesus Christ. As we go through our lives and learn to follow you more fully in our lives, thank you that this written Word will always be there to encourage, to challenge, to guide, and to comfort us in faith. Amen."

TalkSheet #26

LISTENING FOR GOD SPEAKING

1. On the **"You've Got Something Important to Tell Me" Meter**, rate the following by placing them next to 1 for low up to 8 for high on the meter for which of these has something important to say to YOU:

   1_______ 2_______ 3_______ 4_______

   5_______ 6_______ 7_______ 8_______

   a. An advertisement on a billboard you are passing.
   b. A good friend's note passed along in class.
   c. A note from your Dad slipped under your bedroom door.
   d. A birthday card from a relative.
   e. A portion of Scripture you are reading today.
   f. A phone call solicitation.

2. Finish these **Sparkplug Sentences:**

   I listen closer to someone if…

   It is hard for me to pay attention when…

   If I'm going to take something seriously, it had better…

3. **A=Agree, D=Disagree. Circle A for agree and D for disagree.**

Reading the Bible is about listening to God.	A	D
They call it God's Word because God wrote it.	A	D
God speaks to me personally in the Bible.	A	D
God has something to tell me today.	A	D
I would like to know how to read my Bible better.	A	D

4. **What do you suppose is the difference between studying the Bible and listening to the Bible?**

5. **Read 1 Samuel 3:2-10 and consider what Samuel had to do to hear God. What attitude could we adopt from Samuel in our daily lives? (Choose one.)**

   ❐ We could all have more sleepovers in the church.
   ❐ We could take time daily to listen for God.
   ❐ We could ask God to speak to us when we read the Bible.
   ❐ We could go and ask the Eli's in our lives what to do.
   ❐ We could see ourselves as God's servants.
   ❐ We could make Samuel's words to God a part of every prayer we pray.

6. **Try this: Read John 15:14-17. Listen to this passage as though Jesus is saying it to you personally. If this was a conversation, what would you want to say back to Jesus?**

26. LISTENING FOR GOD SPEAKING

THIS WEEK

We are often very good at studying the Bible but not so good at listening to it in our daily lives. Young people can learn an old practice of the church where we sit and listen to the words in Scripture, listening to it as one might listen to the voice of a close friend we trust and want to hear. This is the practice called *Lectio Divina.* In this session we invite the young people to consider what it means to listen to someone we trust, and that we can experience the "voice" of Scripture as time in close friendship of God.

THE OPENER

Ask the following question to get your group members talking and thinking about listening to God through the Bible. Don't worry about the answers since this is a teaser question to get your discussion going: **How difficult is it for you to listen to God speak to you through the Bible?**

DISCUSSION BY THE NUMBERS (Go through the TalkSheet one item at a time.)

1. The purpose of this activity is to explore the notion of written voices: Ones we value greatly and choose to listen to and ones we do not give great value to. The value we give to a written voice depends on whether we feel a connection to the author and desire to hear his "voice" in what is written.
2. Listen to the completed sentences. These sentences will help your group members take a more serious look at listening and paying attention so that later in your discussion you can talk about listening to God.
3. This Agree/Disagree section provides an opportunity for your young people to consider the Word of God as a living voice they can listen to in their lives.
4. Allow the young people to talk together in pairs concerning this question. Then allow each couple to offer their responses. (Note: We study the Word to see what it is saying. This may not be the same thing as listening to it as a vehicle for God to speak to you right now.)
5. Read the Bible text aloud and ask your young people to consider the provided statements and choose one that best represents what they might take from this reading. In this reading from 1 Samuel, God calls the boy Samuel by name, twice. Allow the group time to consider what it means for Samuel to not know God when he calls and the importance of his response in verse 10. Ask, **How does Samuel's response compare with our response to God as we read Scripture?**
6. Here we invite the young people to read a portion of Scripture and listen to it. The exercise asks them to then consider this as a conversation where they can "talk back." Allow each young person time to share.

CLOSING DISCUSSION

We Christians believe that God desires to speak with us personally. One way we read Scripture is to study it and learn *what* it is saying. Another way we read Scripture is to *listen for* God speaking to us personally right now through his Word. Historically this practice is called **Lectio Divina**, or "sacred reading." It is an attitude of reading Scripture where we meet with our divine Friend and really listen for him and to him. Ask, **How might listening to the Bible as God speaking to you today change the way you read the Bible daily?**

CLOSING PRAYER

"Dear Father, you surround us every day with your love and presence. Thank you for desiring to speak to us through your Word. Help us on our part to listen for your voice in your Word. And as we listen, may we grow closer to you this and every day. Amen."

TalkSheet #27

THE HOUSE RULES

1. **GIMME FIVE** rules at school that you feel are important for everyone to follow. What makes a rule a good rule to follow?

   1. ______________________________
   2. ______________________________
   3. ______________________________
   4. ______________________________
   5. ______________________________

2. **Read Psalm 1.** What stands out for you in this reading and how might this psalm relate to living with the house rules?

3. Write down as many of the Ten Commandments as you can remember.

4. Finish these **Sparkplug Sentences:**

   When I think of God's rules for life, it makes me…

   What concerns me most about the Ten Commandments is…

   Rules make me feel…

   One thing I know about God's rules is…

5. **African Bible Study** – Read **John 15:12-17** three times.

   1st Reading – What stands out to you?

   2nd Reading – How does this connect with your world?

   3rd Reading – What do you feel called to do in response?

27. THE HOUSE RULES

THIS WEEK
Young people are faced with rules and regulations all the time, and often the attitude in relation to these rules can be a lack of understanding of why rules can help us live better with each other. Consider the speed limit sign on the road and how often Christians take this law lightly rather than consider it a rule for living together. This session engages young people in considering the "house rules" for living together in this world as given by God: The Ten Commandments.

THE OPENER
Begin by asking the young people to consider and discuss one rule in their own home. Ask the young people to share their home rule by telling what the rule is, who made it, and why they think it is a rule in your home. Ask, "How does this rule help you live together?" Take time to explore with the young people their home rule and why it is important to their family.

DISCUSSION BY THE NUMBERS (Go through the TalkSheet one item at a time.)

1. Ask for your group members to yell out the rules. Ask, Why do you think these rules are necessary or unnecessary? What would happen if these rules did not exist?
2. Ask a group member to reread Psalm 1 out loud for the group. Let several group members share their answers to the question.
3. See how many of the 10 your group members could remember. Read the 10 found in Exodus 20:1-17. Ask, Which of the 10 is your favorite and which is your least favorite?
4. Listen to your group members' responses to the incomplete sentences. This will generate a number of questions you can answer together with your group members.
5. This item can get a faith conversation going about why we should obey Christ.

CLOSING DISCUSSION
Christians believe that God has told us how we should live in relationship with him and with each other in such a way that's pleasing to God. We believe that what is pleasing to God is the best and most loving response to him and to one another. God gave us the Ten Commandments as clear guidelines for living in ways that we can love God with all our heart, mind, and strength, and with love for each other as we love ourselves. Ask, **Why do you think house rules are important in our Christian experience?** Ask, **How do the Ten Commandments protect you?**

CLOSING PRAYER
"Dear Father, we live in this world, but we do not live alone in it. We live here always with you, and we live here with each other. Left to ourselves we might live our lives as it suits us, not knowing or caring how it touches others. Thank you that you remind us and give us clear guidelines on how to live our lives lovingly with all around us. Amen."

TalkSheet #28

ME? DEVELOP A PERSONAL DEVOTIONAL LIFE?

1. Consider the following activities. Place the letter of the activity on the "Difficulty" Scale according to the difficulty of learning that activity.

1________2________3________4________5________
Very Easy Moderate in Difficulty

6________7________8________9________10________
Very Hard

a. Speak a foreign language with confidence.
b. Play a musical piece by Mozart on a violin.
c. Make ice cream from scratch.
d. Use a computer to look up your favorite song.
e. Read the Bible in a year.
f. Recite the Gettysburg Address.

2. Go back to #1. Look at where "read the Bible in a year" fell on the "Difficulty" Scale. What would you have to give up to make this happen?

3. A=Agree, D=Disagree. Circle A for agree and D for disagree.

a. Doing anything well means it becomes a part of your life.	A	D
b. Spending time daily alone with God is important.	A	D
c. Knowing about something is the same as knowing something.	A	D
d. I don't have any more time to do something new.	A	D
e. Reading the Bible every day is too hard.	A	D

4. Finish these Sparkplug Sentences:

If I want to get to know God better, I need to…

To spend time with God every day, I would need to…

Something I could do to improve my relationship with God is…

5. God said, "I will give them a heart to know me, that I am the LORD. They will be my people, and I will be their God, for they will return to me with all their heart" (Jeremiah 24:7). Turn this Bible verse into a prayer in the space below.

28. ME? DEVELOP A PERSONAL DEVOTIONAL LIFE?

THIS WEEK

It's important to all Christians that they understand they can come to know God in their lives. In today's culture where demands on young people's time are so great, young people need to understand that we choose to give time to those things we want to learn how to do. Developing a personal devotional life is a lifetime skill that takes time and commitment, but it is not impossible. We merely need to decide it is important and then give some time daily to developing the skill of spending time with God.

THE OPENER

Ask, **How many hours a week do you spend watching TV? Checking your e-mail or social-networking account? Surfing the Web? Playing Internet games?** Answers to these questions show that your young people have time for a personal devotional life if they choose to make it a priority.

DISCUSSION BY THE NUMBERS (Go through the TalkSheet one item at a time.)

1. In this activity the young people will relate to the concept that developing any skill at any level is possible with a desire and commitment. You may find that some answers vary because of their familiarity or lack of familiarity with the activity as well as a young person's desire to learn that activity. Draw attention to why answers may differ and give time for discussion.
2. Determine what the group members' responses have in common. Talk about how easy it is to make excuses for not reading the Bible.
3. This Agree/Disagree section moves the young people to consider their views about learning to spend time with God every day. Let the young people who agree with a statement go to one side of the room while those who disagree move to the other side. Only then ask them why they agree or disagree with that statement.
4. Ask the young people to finish the incomplete sentences. Each of the three **Sparkplug Sentences** can jumpstart a discussion about what they believe is important if they are going to start spending time daily with God in Scripture and prayer. Point out that each young person may have different issues to consider if beginning a daily devotional habit.
5. Listen to your group members' prayers. What do they all have in common?

CLOSING DISCUSSION

Christians throughout history have understood that one only comes to really know God by spending time with his Word and with him. To know anyone takes a commitment of time spent with that person. Spending time with God daily is about building the most important relationship in our lives. Christians believe we need to spend time with God every day if we are going to get to know him better. Since spending time in God's Word and spending time talking with God are important if we want to know God, we need to develop a daily time when we read the Bible and take time to pray. Ask your group, **If we are going to have a real relationship with God, what do we need to do to build that relationship?** The closing Scripture (Jeremiah 24:7) has an interesting numeric reference. See if they notice it, and point it out if they do not. What does 24/7 suggest to them when they think about having a heart to know God?

CLOSING PRAYER

"Dear Father, we really want to get to know you in our lives. You have given us your Word to know you. You are open to us anytime for a talk, day or night. The question is not whether you are available to be with us, but are we available to spend time to be alone with you. We might not even be sure where or how to begin. But we know that anything worth learning how to do begins with a desire to do it. Help us develop a habit of personal time with you. Amen."

But as for me, I watch in hope for the LORD, I wait for God my Savior; my God will hear me. **(Micah 7:7)**

Introduce the Topic

Allow Enough Time

AFFIRM ALL RESPONSES—RIGHT OR WRONG

Don't Be the Authoritative Answer

LISTEN TO EACH PERSON

Don't Force It

Don't Take Sides

LET THEM LAUGH!

Allow Silence

BE CREATIVE AND FLEXIBLE

Be There for Your Kids

TalkSheet #29

WHAT IS SALVATION?

1. Rate the following on the "Push the Restart, Please!" Scale. Place the letter of each situation on the line.

1________2________3________4________5________
Not yet Not sure Maybe

6________7________8________9________10________
Good idea Restart now!

a. Your parents caught you in an embarrassing moment.
b. You forgot to study and the test begins now.
c. You are sent to the school office because of something you said.
d. Your best friend won't speak to you because of a prank.
e. You spent all your money on something that is suddenly obsolete.
f. While playing a sport your shorts fall down.

2. Freed From/Freed For: List three per side of what you think salvation frees you from and frees you for.

Freed From: Freed For:

______________________________/______________________________

______________________________/______________________________

______________________________/______________________________

3. **Read Ephesians 2:8-10. What is important for you to remember about salvation from this reading? (Choose one.)**

- ☐ Faith in what God is doing in Jesus is a big part of my salvation.
- ☐ Even the fact that I can trust God is a gift from God.
- ☐ The fact that faith saves me is still God's doing alone.
- ☐ No one can really brag about being a Christian.
- ☐ We are saved for a purpose.
- ☐ God is still working in me.
- ☐ Being saved means God has something good for us to do.

4. Finish these Sparkplug Sentences:

The important thing about salvation to me is…

I think salvation is about…

When someone asks, "Are you saved?" I would say…

5. African Bible Study – Read Romans 8:1-2 three times and respond following each reading.

1st Reading – What stands out to you?

2nd Reading – How does this connect with your world?

3rd Reading – What do you feel called to do in response?

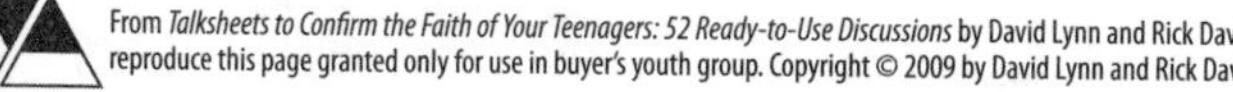

29. WHAT IS SALVATION?

THIS WEEK

Young people often hear the church word *salvation* and wonder what it means. Essentially salvation is the gift of God, a process by which God draws us into relationship with him. Through the process of salvation we are saved from sin and the consequences of sin and freed to experience the love and the power of God in our lives. Through salvation God establishes a new and lasting relationship with us that leads to glory.

THE OPENER

Begin by asking your young people to consider and discuss what it means to have a fresh start and whether they have witnessed someone actually enjoying a fresh start in their lives. Ask, **What does it mean when someone says "I want to have a fresh start"? Have you ever witnessed someone in your life who got a fresh start? What was it like for them?** Close this time by leading into a connection with the topic of salvation by asking, **How is the idea of a fresh start similar to salvation?**

DISCUSSION BY THE NUMBERS (Go through the TalkSheet one item at a time.)

1. Ask the young people to rate the following situations they might encounter on the "**Push the Restart, Please!" Scale**. Have them place the letter of the situation on the scale according to whether they would like to have the "restart button" pushed to have the opportunity to do things differently with different consequences. Allow two minutes for them to rate each situation and then discuss their responses.
2. This can be difficult for young people because it requires them to think beyond the Sunday school answer. Talk about how your group members' lives are affected by salvation as it frees us from something and frees us for something else.
3. Read the Bible text aloud and ask your young people to consider the provided statements and choose the one that best expresses what they believe this text tells them about salvation. And find out why.
4. Ask the young people to finish the incomplete sentences. These **Sparkplug Sentences** get personal about salvation and will generate questions you can answer together with your group.
5. Use this item to dig deeper with your group into the meaning of **Romans 8:1-2**.

CLOSING DISCUSSION

Christians believe that salvation is a gift from God that frees us from the past and the power of sin and separation from God in our lives. We believe that it frees us to live in the love and power of knowing God in our lives now and forever. While it is God alone who saves, we need to live *into* what he gives us if we are to experience salvation. It means we are to *live* as if we are saved. We are to believe it and then experience it in our daily lives. We are to live as if it is true because it *is* true! Ask, **Why is a fresh start an important aspect of the Christian experience?**

CLOSING PRAYER

"Dear Father, in Jesus Christ you have freed us from sin. You have freed us to experience your love and your power in our lives through salvation in Jesus Christ. Help us to live in this salvation and enjoy this new and lasting relationship we have with you. Amen."

TalkSheet #30

THE FALL

How Did It All Get This Way, Anyway?

1. **GIMME FIVE** indicators in your school or culture that demonstrate we are all broken in our relationship with God.

   1. ______________________________
   2. ______________________________
   3. ______________________________
   4. ______________________________
   5. ______________________________

2. Rate each phrase on the **"Legends of the Fall" Scale** according to how much they were the result of the fall of humanity.

   1_______2_______3_______4_______5_______6_______7_______8_______9_______10_______

   Not really — Could be — Most likely — Fallen

   a. Rise in divorce rate and broken families.
   b. Recreational drug use.
   c. Poor cafeteria food.
   d. Violent crimes.
   e. Low grades in school.
   f. The Beatles breaking up.

3. **Read Genesis 3:1-13.** What changed in their relationship with God? In what ways can you tell this change is still at work today?

4. Finish these **Sparkplug Sentences:**

   I notice the results of the fall in me when I…

   One thing that is clear about all people is that…

   What confuses me about the fall is…

5. **African Bible Study** – Read **Romans 5:18-19** three times and respond following each reading.

   1st Reading – What stands out to you?

   2nd Reading – How does this connect with your world?

   3rd Reading – What do you feel called to do in response?

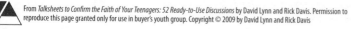

30. THE FALL: How Did It All Get This Way, Anyway?

THIS WEEK

The church speaks about the fall as the beginning of the problem we all share in our relationship with God. The term *fall* can describe the first sin by Adam and Eve recorded in Genesis as the initiating act that has established a stronghold in the lives of humanity to this very day. All humanity is affected as a whole, as well as each individual personally. The ruin of self-centeredness and disobedience has penetrated us all, in all aspects of our lives. As a drop of poison effectively poisons the entire glass of water, so the act of Adam (and our continual complicity with it) poisons our relationship with God and with each other.

THE OPENER

Read the following sentence and then ask your group to decide which of the four choices are correct.

Most people I know think people are basically…

a. good and always want to do the right thing.
b. neutral and the direction they go (good or bad) depends upon how they are raised.
c. bad and often sin against God.
d. I'm clueless.

Some of your group members may express the belief that people are basically good. Go easy on these group members. This is a common belief in our culture—a belief that ignores history—but must be expressed if people are going to live autonomously and independently from our Creator God, who has a claim on all our lives. Original sin/the fall/our sinful nature is a historic belief of Christianity—and is the one empirically verifiable belief of our faith. We can't prove there is a God, but we can easily demonstrate the sinfulness of humankind. Just look at man's inhumanity to man in the last 100 years!

DISCUSSION BY THE NUMBERS (Go through the TalkSheet one item at a time.)

1. Ask your group to list five indicators they see in their school or in our culture that demonstrate to them we are all broken in our relationship with God. Talk together about a common trait your group members have noticed that expresses our self-centered and disobedient nature in relationship with God. While this may be an uncomfortable discussion, it is important that young people notice the ways we live out the fall in our daily lives and demonstrate we are broken in our relationship with almighty God.
2. This gives you a fun way to talk further about the fall and our broken relationship with God.
3. **Genesis 3:1-13** begins humankind's long history of rebellion against a holy God. It was the risk God took in giving people free will. It was at this point human sin and evil entered the world and radically shifted our relationship with God. This broken relationship required human death. Fortunately, God planned for our redemption through Christ. While we still must die, our faith in Christ gives us a way out from sin.
4. Listen to your group members' responses and answer together any of the inevitable questions that will arise as a result of this activity.
5. Read **Romans 5:18-19** aloud slowly to your group. Then let them answer the three questions. Talk about what makes us acceptable to God.

CLOSING DISCUSSION

Christians believe that the term "the fall" refers not only to the first sinful act in Scripture, but also to the tainting effect of that sin upon all humanity as all live out the nature of that original sin in our lives. Not only was all humanity affected, but every person individually has been and is distorted by sin. Like one drop of poison taints a whole glass of water, so the fall has infected humanity as a whole and each person individually in every aspect of our lives. Even our good acts are tainted by selfish desires for recognition. It all began with one act of selfish disobedience that we propagate every day in our lives. Ask, **If we're all affected by the fall, what's God's answer to the fall?**

CLOSING PRAYER

"Dear Father, we all experience daily the lingering sin that lives in our lives. We know it all started somewhere. What is worse is we all keep it going in our world today. Thank you for not giving up on us and for answering our brokenness with your love and mercy in Jesus. Amen."

1. What does the X on a shopping mall map tell you?

2. Circle the one activity below that you would rank as the most important in your life right now.

a. Smoking marijuana every day
b. Looking good all the time
c. Needing a personal devotion time daily
d. Never missing an episode of my favorite program
e. Being a part of all youth group activities
f. Never being tardy to class
g. Playing Internet games daily
h. Earning money for a car
i. Other: ______________________________

3. Read Romans 3:22-24. List three things you feel you would want to remember from this reading.

1. ______________________________

2. ______________________________

3. ______________________________

4. Finish these Sparkplug Sentences:

To me sin is all about…

Where I notice sin at work in my life is…

I think the hardest thing to understand about sin is…

5. African Bible Study – Read 1 John 1:6-10 three times and respond following each reading.

1st Reading – What stands out to you?

2nd Reading – How does this connect with your world?

3rd Reading – What do you feel called to do in response?

31. SIN: "X" Marks the Spot

THIS WEEK

Understanding the nature of sin in our lives is an important aspect of the Christian experience. Often young people are not clear how sin expresses to us the truth of where we are in relationship to God. This session presents discussion points that suggest that knowing the sense of sin in our lives indicates where we are in relationship to God.

THE OPENER

Begin by asking the following two questions that look at the health of relationships. These two questions will get your group members thinking about relationships in general as you move into a discussion of their relationship with God. Ask, **What are your three most important relationships? How do you know the health of these relationships?**

DISCUSSION BY THE NUMBERS (Go through the TalkSheet one item at a time.)

1. Mall maps usually have a marker with an "X" that indicates where you are in the mall. This is helpful in understanding where we are and where we want to be. Ask, **How does this relate to the topic of understanding sin and our relationship with God?**
2. The one circled activity indicates where someone gives her greatest energy in life. What gets our greatest energy usually shows where we are—where our X is, if you will. Ask your group to consider the following: If sin causes you to be self-centered, then where do you need to be headed based on this activity?
3. Listen to your group members' three responses. Ask the group to decide which of the responses is the most important.
4. Listen to your group members' completed sentences. This activity usually brings up questions you can answer as a group.
5. Read **1 John 1:6-10** again and listen to your group's responses.

CLOSING DISCUSSION

Christians believe that understanding our sin, our broken relationship with God, and how we live out that brokenness needs to be acknowledged, realized, and faced head-on if we are going to experience God's forgiveness and have a close fellowship with him through Jesus. Understanding the nature of sin is one way God helps us to know where we are in relationship to him. Ask, **How broken is your relationship with God?** Ask, **Why do you think it is important for God to replace the big "I" in the center of our lives for the Christian experience?**

CLOSING PRAYER

"Dear Father, we are troubled by how our lives are so self-centered. It is hard not to live with a big 'I' in the center of our lives. But thank you that through Jesus we have a new way to live in relationship with you and with each other. Thank you that SIN, my big 'I,' does not have to rule in my life. Amen."

TalkSheet #32

ATONEMENT

The Sin Cure

1. When was the last time you stood up for someone else?

- I have never stood up for anyone, not even myself.
- I have never stood up for anyone else, only myself.
- I remember a time I stood up for someone else. It was when I…

2. Ask, **How difficult is it to fall short of God's standard, to need God to stand up for us?**

- You gotta be a real loser to fall short.
- Only girls fall short since Eve sinned first.
- Not hard at all since everyone falls short of God's standard for any sin they commit.

Romans 3:23 tells us everyone comes up short.

3. **A=Agree, D=Disagree.** Circle **A** for agree and **D** for disagree.

a. In God's eyes there are good people and bad people in the world.	A	D
b. Some people need the Savior more than others.	A	D
c. When it comes to sin, we are all in the same boat.	A	D
d. Jesus stands in my place so I can stand with God.	A	D
e. The only one who can make anyone right with God is Jesus.	A	D

4. *Atonement* is a theological word that means to do something to keep a sin or sins from being held against a person. God requires death to atone for sin—that's because sin is serious in the eyes of a holy God. Humankind doesn't take sin so seriously because it is so common. In the Old Testament, people of faith had to sacrifice, or kill, an animal to "atone" for their sins. Almighty God would look at this sacrifice and remember that Jesus would pay the ultimate sacrifice, or death, for sin. On the line below write one question you have about atonement.

____

5. Finish these **Sparkplug Sentences:**

When I think that Jesus stood up for me, I think…

Something I don't get about Jesus is…

If I were to tell someone about Jesus, I would tell…

6. Read, listen, and in one sentence put each of the four Bible readings in your own words.

John 3:16 ______________________________

Isaiah 53:5 ______________________________

1 Peter 1:18-19 ______________________________

Romans 8:3 ______________________________

32. ATONEMENT: The Sin Cure

THIS WEEK

An essential understanding of the Christian faith is that through Jesus we are healed of our sin and separation from God. It is the act of atonement in Christ that provides what God requires for our sin. In a real sense, it is God who provides a cure for sin by providing himself what is needed to heal what holds us apart. God stands up for us and in Christ takes the consequence of sin in order that we might live in relationship with him.

THE OPENER

Ask, **What is the first thing you think of when you hear the word *cross*?**

DISCUSSION BY THE NUMBERS (Go through the TalkSheet one item at a time.)

1. This question gets your group to consider what it means that in Christ, God stands up for them and in fact takes their punishment in their place.
2. **Romans 3:23** gives the answer. Ask a young person to read this passage out loud. Then discuss its significance.
3. These Agree/Disagree statements allow your young people to consider sin and the need for the Savior. Allow each young person to respond by choosing sides of your meeting area to be an Agree side and a Disagree side. Allow young people to tell why they agree or disagree.
4. Listen to the questions your group members have about atonement. Try to answer the questions as a group. Any unanswered questions can be taken to your congregation's pastor.
5. Listen to the completed sentences that'll keep your discussion of sin and atonement going.
6. Ask for volunteers to read their summaries.

CLOSING DISCUSSION

Christians believe that all have fallen short of God's standards and that everyone is lost in sin. God's only sure provision for us is provided in Jesus. We believe that Jesus takes our sins upon himself and that through his blood we are made whole in God's sight. Jesus is God's cure for our separation from him. Ask, **If God has provided a remedy for what ails our relationship, what is it we might need to do?**

CLOSING PRAYER

"Dear loving Father, we are so amazed at how much you love us. While we were yet sinners, you gave us a way out of our sin and back to you. Thank you for Jesus' gift and for the atonement he makes for all of us. Amen."

TalkSheet #33

REPENTANCE

Turning from "Whatever!" to God

1. Read Luke 15:11-20. How did the son change his mind and turn away from one thing and toward another? (You can check more than one answer.)

- ❐ The son decided to mooch off his dad again.
- ❐ His life hit a bottom and there seemed to be nowhere else to go.
- ❐ He was ready for a change of scenery.
- ❐ After living life on his own terms, the son realized his way didn't work.
- ❐ He missed his brother.
- ❐ He got tired of the fun where he was and wanted to go back home.
- ❐ He was bored.

2. Consider the following on the "That Would Change My Mind" Scale by placing the letter of the event on the scale that would determine how likely you would be to change.

1_______2_______3_______4_______5_______6_______7_______8_______9_______10_______

Not likely — Well, maybe — You got my attention — I'm turning!

a. It's against the law.

b. Your dad tells you to "stop it right now!"

c. The Bible says clearly that doing this is wrong.

d. Your friends think you are stupid if you do it.

e. Something inside you tells you it is wrong.

f. Television ads speak out against it.

3. Read Luke 15:20-24. What did the father do in response to the son's return? (You may check more than one answer.)

- ❐ He changed the locks on the doors.
- ❐ He ran out to meet him and welcome him home.
- ❐ He finally found a good reason to kill that fatted calf.
- ❐ He brought his son fully home by making it clear he was his son.
- ❐ He dressed him up so that no one would see how bad he looked.
- ❐ He was so overwhelmed with joy he couldn't do anything else but throw a party.
- ❐ He found out his other son was also lost and needed his help.

4. Finish these Sparkplug Sentences:

Repentance means you need to…

The story of the son and his father makes me think about…

Jesus told this story so that I would know…

5. "Let the wicked forsake his way and the evil man his thoughts. Let him turn to the LORD, and he will have mercy on him, and to our God, for he will freely pardon" (Isaiah 55:7). What do you think God is telling us here?

33. REPENTANCE: Turning from "Whatever!" to God

THIS WEEK

The notion of repentance is an important aspect in a young Christian's life as one turns from something and turns to God. It is not only a matter of saying no to harmful things in our lives. We need to also say yes to something else. As we explore the parable of the son who left home and the father who receives him back, we look at the way the son's thinking changes and how he remembers home. As we return to the Father, we can turn away from those things that are not pleasing to him. We need to learn that repentance is also turning *to* something that really matters. As the son remembered his father's house and how he treated his servants, we can remember our Father's love and turn to him.

THE OPENER

Begin by asking your group to remember a time when they changed their mind about something. Ask them to consider this process as two steps. They first must turn away from something and then turn toward something. When we change our mind about anything, we let something go and we pick up something new. This discussion will set the groundwork for the young people to consider repentance as a turning from and a turning to.

DISCUSSION BY THE NUMBERS (Go through the TalkSheet one item at a time.)

1. Have your young people consider how the son changed his mind and turned from something to something; again, emphasize the process of turning from and turning to as seen in the story. Ask, **What changed his mind and how did he act on the change?**
2. Discuss each influence and where your group members placed it on the scale. Ask, **What would most influence you to change your mind and repent?**
3. Read the Bible text aloud and ask your young people to choose statements that are true. Ask them to defend their choices. Ask, **What surprised you about the father's response?**
4. Listen to the completed sentences and together explore questions that arise.
5. Ask, **How is this like the father who received the son home?**

CLOSING DISCUSSION

Christians believe that repentance is an important part of our Christian experience. When we turn to Jesus we are also often turning from something else that can lead us away from getting to know him and follow him better. Repentance is when we say, "Father, you are right." And we turn from our way of doing life to his way. Repentance is not a one-time event. Repentance is a lifelong journey where we are always turning to God. Ask, **Why is repentance an important part of the Christian experience? How often do you think you need to repent?**

CLOSING PRAYER

"Dear loving and receiving Father, there is so much in life that calls for us and can lead us away from you. If we find ourselves far from you, no matter where we are or how far, help us remember your love, remember how you care for us, and have the courage to look around, stand up, and turn back around to you. Amen."

TalkSheet #34

CONFESSION

1. Rate the following on the "Need-to-Share-It" Scale:

1________2________3________4________5________
Keep It Private — Might Share

6________7________8________9________10________
Could Share — Gotta Tell!

a. You received a ticket for speeding.
b. A close friend of yours just got grounded for coming in late.
c. You just had a terrible fight with your best friend.
d. A close friend's parents are getting a divorce.
e. You cheated on an exam at school and feel bad.
f. You lied to a friend about something important.

2. Read Psalm 32:3-5. What did the psalmist do and how did God respond? (Check all that are true.)

Psalmist:
- ❒ Complained all day long
- ❒ Kept silent about his sin
- ❒ Felt really bad deep inside
- ❒ Took a long holiday to Spain
- ❒ Admitted his wrongdoing to God

God:
- ❒ Said "I told you so"
- ❒ Found a better way to punish him
- ❒ Forgave him
- ❒ Got really angry and did not speak to him
- ❒ Still loved him

3. Finish these Sparkplug Sentences:

One thing that can break up a relationship is…

An important part of a good relationship is…

One thing I think God wants from me in our relationship is…

4. Be prepared to talk about a time you were afraid to confess a sin to a parent, to a friend, to a teacher, or to God. You don't have to talk about the specific sin but rather what you were feeling inside and what those feelings were doing to you.

5. African Bible Study – Read 1 John 1:9 three times, stopping each time to reflect.

1st Reading – What stands out in this verse for you?

2nd Reading – How do you connect with this verse?

3rd Reading – What do you feel this text is calling you to do?

34. CONFESSION

THIS WEEK

Confession is an important part of our relationship with God, and young people can misunderstand the nature of confession. Confession is important for Christians to keep an honest perspective in our relationship with God. But so often we keep our real concerns hidden, silent, burying them deep in our minds and hearts as if we can keep them far from the healing presence of Jesus. Christians believe there is power available to us in Jesus when we confess our sins.

THE OPENER

Ask your group members to consider a time when they needed to get something off their chests. Ask, **Why was it important to get it off your chest? How important was it to be honest?**

DISCUSSION BY THE NUMBERS (Go through the TalkSheet one item at a time.)

1. Follow up by asking, **Is it gossip or confession? What is the difference?**
2. Read the Psalm text aloud and ask your young people **How do you relate to this Psalm personally?**
3. Listen to the completed sentences for questions the group members have and then answer these questions as a group.
4. Holding our sins inside without confessing them is harmful. Listen for what these feelings have done to your group members. Share what has happened to you when you have withheld your confession.
5. Ask, **Why do you think we should celebrate the fact that God lets us confess our sins and then wipes those sins away?**

CLOSING DISCUSSION

Christians believe that God loves and forgives us in Jesus Christ. But forgives us from what? We believe sin is big and takes shape in many little ways in our daily lives. Being honest with ourselves and with God is one way we help keep our relationship clear and open. Confession, admitting to God openly, is one way we keep our relationship healthy. Ask, **Why do you feel confession is an important part of the Christian experience? When was the last time you confessed your sins to God? How tough is it to admit your sins to God? To yourself? To another human being?**

CLOSING PRAYER

"Dear loving Father, you desire us to be in relationship with you and for that relationship to be honest and open. You invite us to confess to you, to speak to you openly about how sin may be working in our lives. We know you forgive us. We know you already know what we are going to share before we share it. Yet we also know it is important for us to be honest with you and with ourselves. Help us to live open to your presence. Amen."

1. When Karl Barth, a famous German theologian, came to America, he was asked, "When were you converted (when did you become a Christian)?" His response went something like this: "I remember it was on an afternoon in 30 or so A.D. when Jesus died on a cross." What do you think of Karl Barth's response to the conversion question?

2. **A=Agree, D=Disagree.** Circle A for agree and D for disagree.

Conversion happens at some point in everyone who believes.	A	D
Real conversion changes everything you believe about God.	A	D
A conversion makes you a new creation.	A	D
Conversion is something God alone does in you.	A	D
A conversion usually happens is similar ways in people.	A	D
Most conversions are evident when they occur.	A	D

3. A young person is automatically a Christian if one or both of his parents are Christians! (Circle one.)

TRUE FALSE I DON'T KNOW

4. Finish these **Sparkplug Sentences:**

One area of my life where I have noticed a turning point is…

I think a conversion makes a person new in that…

When someone turns from something and turns toward God, they…

5. **Read Luke 19:1-10.** How do you know Zacchaeus experienced a conversion? When do you think this man became a Christian?

35. CONVERSION

THIS WEEK

Conversion is an important part of the Christian experience that young people are often worried or confused about. The influence in our culture and in the lives of young people to "fit in" pressures youth to want to express similar experiences, or to be fearful of sharing personal experiences. It is important for young people to understand that while conversion is an important part of the Christian experience, all Christians have not experienced conversion in the same way. All youth may have different experiences with conversion. Allowing a format to discuss conversion openly will help young people come to terms with the nature of this part of the journey of faith.

THE OPENER

What is the first thing that comes to your mind when you hear the word *conversion*?

DISCUSSION BY THE NUMBERS (Go through the TalkSheet one item at a time.)

1. Ask, **Do you remember the day you were converted? Do you have to remember it?**
2. Explore with your young people the reasoning behind their responses. Note that while their responses may be the same, the reasoning behind their responses may vary. Explore these differences with the young people.
3. This statement is false. God has no grandparents. But this statement can get a great faith conversation going about what exactly makes up conversion.
4. Listen to the completed sentences. As questions arise (as they often do with **Sparkplug Sentences**) answer them as a group.
5. Zacchaeus' conversion is a fascinating account because there was such a stark contrast to his life. As a tax collector he ripped off his own people of large sums of money to give some of it to Rome as taxes. He had the support of the Roman army to enforce the collection of money. Once he met Jesus his life did a spectacular 180. Many of us, at least those of us who grew up in Christian homes, have not had this sort of conversion experience, yet we still needed to turn from our sins and give our lives to Christ.

CLOSING DISCUSSION

Christians believe that a turning point in the process of our salvation through Jesus Christ is conversion, where we have a deep realization and turn from something that pulls us away from God and faithfulness and to God and a deeper relationship with him. While conversion happens at some point in the lives of every believer, Jesus deals with us all on levels that are personal, and so the Christian experience of conversion can be quite different for every person as we turn to a closer walk with our Lord. Ask, **How is conversion an important part of the Christian experience? When do you think you experienced conversion?**

CLOSING PRAYER

"Dear Father, you come to us and move us to respond to your presence, your Word, and your love. You move us to turn toward you, and that means that as we step into a new living relationship with you, we also step into a new relationship with everything around us. We see our lives and our world with new eyes. You convert us so our way of thinking is more in step with your Good News. Thank you. Amen."

TalkSheet #36

FORGIVENESS

God's Way Is Our Way Out

1. **Consider the following situations and rate them on the "Get Over It" Scale by placing the letter of the situation on the line according to what you think would be your ability to get over it:**

   1________2________3________4________5________
   No problem Some problem

   6________7________8________9________10________
   This will be tough Never

   a. A neighbor kid steals something of yours you left outside.
   b. A student at school texts a message with a rumor about you.
   c. A friend lies to you about where he was last night.
   d. A boy bumps into you at the theater, and you drop your popcorn.
   e. A drunk driver hits a member of your family.
   f. A woman at the grocery store gives you the wrong change.

2. **A=Agree, D=Disagree. Circle A for agree and D for disagree.**

a. People who have been forgiven are better at forgiving others.	A	D
b. To err is human; to forgive is something only God can do.	A	D
c. Forgiveness tells someone who hurt you it is okay.	A	D
d. Sometimes the only way out of a bad situation is forgiveness.	A	D
e. Forgiveness is extremely important to Jesus.	A	D

3. **Describe a time you witnessed an act of forgiveness.**

4. **Finish these Sparkplug Sentences:**

   When I think about forgiveness, I wish I knew…

   Something I find most difficult about forgiving someone is…

   When I think about God forgiving me again and again and again, it makes me want to…

5. **Read Matthew 18:23-33. What is this passage saying to you about forgiveness?**

   - ❒ You can just forget it, mister.
   - ❒ Forgiveness received by God should change the way we see others.
   - ❒ To actually be forgiven we have to live like we already are forgiven.
   - ❒ God has given something wonderful to be shared.
   - ❒ Forgiveness is a state of mind.
   - ❒ How we live with the gift of forgiveness matters to God.

36. FORGIVENESS: God's Way Is Our Way Out

THIS WEEK

One of the most important teachings of the Christian church is the miracle of forgiveness. Christians understand we are forgiven an incredible debt by God through Jesus on the cross. Forgiveness, or letting go of a right to get even and carrying the hurt in a new way, is how God handled our sin. Jesus also teaches that as people who know the forgiveness of God, we are "bound to show the same kind of mercy" to others that God shows us. How many times should we show this kind of mercy? When Peter asked this of Jesus, Jesus answered him, "I do not say to you, up to seven times, but up to seventy times seven" (**Matthew 18:22 NASB**). While the nature of how one forgives is an important lesson to learn, all Christians realize that forgiveness is not an option. We need to be committed to what God is committed to.

THE OPENER

Begin with this question: **Is it easier to forgive or be forgiven?**

DISCUSSION BY THE NUMBERS (Go through the TalkSheet one item at a time.)

1. The purpose of this activity is to engage your young people with the notion of forgiveness as an important part of the Christian experience, not only as we read it from Scripture, but also as we live our faith in the day-to-day world.
2. This Agree/Disagree section offers the young people a time to consider forgiveness and how it plays out in daily life in their relationship with God and with others. Examine how your group members feel about forgiveness. Check out how relevant forgiveness is in how they deal with difficult situations.
3. Invite the young people to remember a situation where they witnessed an act of forgiveness. Telling the story of such an event can help relate to how forgiveness takes shape in our daily lives. Ask, **What about this made it an act of forgiveness?**
4. Listen to the completed sentences. Answer together any questions that arise.
5. Ask your young people to choose a statement that best expresses what they will remember from the reading. Then it can be fun and instructional at the same time to have your young people act out this parable. Assign each character in the story and the part of the narrator to individuals in the group. After the story has been acted, ask, **What strikes you as wrong in this story?** and **How could the forgiven servant have acted that may have shown he really got what the king had done for him?** (Important historical note to share: "Ten thousand" is translated from the Greek word *murios*, from which we get our word "myriad" as in "myriad (or countless number of) stars." A talent was the largest measure of weight in Jewish commerce. The servant owed "a countless number multiplied by the largest weight of something." A denarius was a typical day's wage for a worker. One hundred denarii is almost four months' wages and is no small sum or "a few dollars," but a real debt.

CLOSING DISCUSSION

Christians believe forgiveness is a big deal because it is a big deal to Jesus. We believe that not only does God forgive us, but that part of being forgiven means living it out in our lives. Forgiveness takes hard work and doesn't guarantee that everything will get better. Being forgiven is almost impossible unless you believe and experience the power of it in your life. Christians believe the best way to express we are forgiven is to be forgivers.

Ask your group, **Why do you think God wants us to be serious about forgiving others?** Before the closing prayer, remind the young people forgiveness matters so much to Jesus he told us to pray about it. (**Important note**: By praying, "Forgive us our sins as we forgive the sins of others," we are to forgive like God forgives us. Ask, **How big a forgiver are you?**)

CLOSING PRAYER

Close by praying the Lord's Prayer.

1. **What do you do when you make a mistake writing a paper? How important is it to be able to erase mistakes?**

2. **What would happen if we didn't have the ability to erase our mistakes? (Choose one that best speaks for you.)**

   a. The earth would cease to exist as we know it.
   b. Life would get really messy and complicated.
   c. We would soon run out of space from all the trash we would produce.
   d. There would be no room in my closet to hide all the mistakes.
   e. I would feel really vulnerable and silly in front of others.

3. Finish these **Sparkplug Sentences:**

   When God forgives me, he treats me just as if…

   When I realize I have sinned, I can…

   When God sees me today, to him I look just as if I'd…

4. **Read Luke 18:9-14. What happened in this story that matters most to you?**

5. **African Bible Study** – Read **Romans 3:22-24** three times, stopping to reflect after each reading.

   1st Reading – What stands out in this verse for you?

   2nd Reading – How do you connect with this verse?

   3rd Reading – What do you feel this text is calling you to do?

37. JUSTIFIED

THIS WEEK

Some church words are difficult to understand, let alone get a sense of how they might express something relevant to our daily lives. *Justification* is one of those words. It is important to see how this word expresses an essential aspect of our relationship with God. God is the One who justifies us through the act of Jesus on the cross. His saving act forgives us of our sins, but how does that relate to justification? Because of forgiveness in Christ, God treats us just as if we had never sinned. We now are "usable" again. We now are relatable again. A relationship has been reestablished and the page has been wiped clean.

THE OPENER

Check out how many of your youth group members can define the word *justification*.

DISCUSSION BY THE NUMBERS (Go through the TalkSheet one item at a time.)

1. When we erase a mistake, whether we use the backspace key on our computer or a pencil eraser, we are given the opportunity to act as if the mistake had never happened. This is what justification is all about.
2. Ask the question and have your young people discuss one statement that best speaks for them. Then share your responses and why it speaks for you.
3. An important point to make about the first sentence: *Justified* means "Just-as-If-I'd Never Sinned." To help your young people understand the notion of being justified by God, say it slowly to create **just as if I'd**… Say, **When God justifies me in Christ, he treats me *Just as if I'd*...never sinned!**
4. Gather the various perspectives of your group members about **Luke 18:9-14**. Ask, **Which of the two individuals in the story are you most like? Do you think God would say he is pleased with you?**
5. Find out what your group members learned from reading and listening to **Romans 3:22-24**.

CLOSING DISCUSSION

Justification is an important aspect of our new relationship with God because of Jesus. Justification allows me to openly relate to God as if I had never sinned against God at all. Through Jesus, God erases my sin and treats me just as if I had never sinned. This gives me an opportunity each day to live as if I had never made a mistake. Ask, **What is important to you about justification in your Christian experience? How could this idea of justification help you live the Christian life differently?**

CLOSING PRAYER

"Dear Father, thank you for not throwing us away and starting again, but erasing our sins and making us useful again as your children, by giving us an opportunity to live like it was before we ever did anything wrong. As you have justified us and as you treat us in a new way, may we learn how to forgive others and treat them again as useful. Amen."

TalkSheet #38

SANCTIFICATION

God at Work IN You

1. **GIMME FIVE** ways you have grown the past two years to be a stronger member of your family, congregation, or school.

    1. ______________________________
    2. ______________________________
    3. ______________________________
    4. ______________________________
    5. ______________________________

2. Rate the following statements on the **"I Wanna Be" Scale.** Place the letter of the statement on the scale according to how it stands for you.

1_____2_____3_____4_____5_____6_____7_____8_____9_____10_____
No Way! — Maybe I Could Do That — That's for Me!

"I wanna be…"

a. really cool at school.
b. someone who knows how to pray.
c. successful in business.
d. just like Jesus.
e. a rock star.
f. rich and famous.
g. someone who puts others before self.
h. a sports star.
i. a leader in my congregation.
j. someone who gets whatever I want.

3. **Read Romans 8:29.** What is clearly God's intention for all of us? (Check each one you think is true.)

- To grow our hair out and try to dress like Jesus
- To have a large family
- To make everything end up like he wants it to be
- To shape us from the inside into people who are very like Jesus
- To think every day, "What would Jesus do?"
- To change us into his children
- To have Jesus be the gold standard for what children are to be

4. **Three for Three.** Give three ways you are growing as a person of God and three ways you have yet to grow:

Growing
1. ______________________________
2. ______________________________
3. ______________________________

Need to Grow
1. ______________________________
2. ______________________________
3. ______________________________

5. Finish these **Sparkplug Sentences:**

One way I would like to grow more like Jesus is…

For me to grow deeper in faith I need to…

One thing about sanctification that is really cool is…

6. **African Bible Study** – Read **Philippians 2:12-13** three times, stopping each time to reflect.

1st Reading – What stands out to you?

2nd Reading – How does this connect with your world?

3rd Reading – What do you feel called to do in response?

38. SANCTIFICATION: God at Work IN You

THIS WEEK

Sanctification is a key area of the Christian experience many young people do not understand. Often we convey the Christian faith as a moral religion where we are to muster our own ability to be holy. Scripture makes it quite clear that without God's assistance we are all unable to walk a life worthy of God. God's activity in our lives works to shape our lives and our living to reflect his love and his presence. While this can be a slow process (or in some cases fast), it is God who works to glorify himself in the lives of his people.

THE OPENER

Begin by asking this question: **When was the last time you thought about your sanctification?**

DISCUSSION BY THE NUMBERS (Go through the TalkSheet one item at a time.)

1. As we grow up, we take our place as responsible members in the vital relationships in our lives. So, too, with being a part of the body of Christ, except it is God who "grows us up" into the likeness of his Son, Jesus Christ.
2. This activity gets your group talking about where they want to go in life. Explore what price you must pay for each of these goals. Ask, **Which of these will give you a meaningful and purpose-filled life?**
3. Read the Bible text aloud and ask your young people to discuss their answers. This text from Paul's letter to the Romans is a key statement expressing God's intention to create children who are in the image of his first Son, Jesus. It expresses that God's presence in our lives has a purpose and an outcome. We will all be transformed by his grace to ultimately become a family whose likeness is that of God's Son, Jesus.
4. Ask volunteers to share their lists. When each one is finished, ask them to consider the closing question of this exercise—"Which side are you on?" This question asks which area of their lives are they placing most of their attention or energy in?
5. Listen to the completed sentences. Together as a group answer any questions that arise.
6. This Bible passage from **Philippians 2:12-13** speaks specifically about sanctification. We were saved (conversion), are being saved (sanctification, or growing more like Jesus), and will be saved (in the future we will be given eternal life).

CLOSING DISCUSSION

Christians believe that God works within us to remove our stubbornness toward him and make us want to have a friendship with him (**Ezekiel 11:19**). God gently moves in our lives and our thoughts, our intentions and our actions to create in us a life that reflects his presence and his love. Sanctification—to be made holy—is a part of the Christian experience with God. Ask, **What stands out for you about sanctification?**

CLOSING PRAYER

"Dear Father, you love us just the way we are. Thank you. And yet you promise to not leave us the way we are. Thank you. Mold us, shape us, move us, fashion us—each and every day—to be more like Jesus and to be a reflection of your love and your presence. In such a way we grow to honor you. Amen."

SECTION 7 QUESTIONS ABOUT DISCIPLESHIP

I am the good shepherd. I know my own and my own know me. **(John 10:14 ISV)**

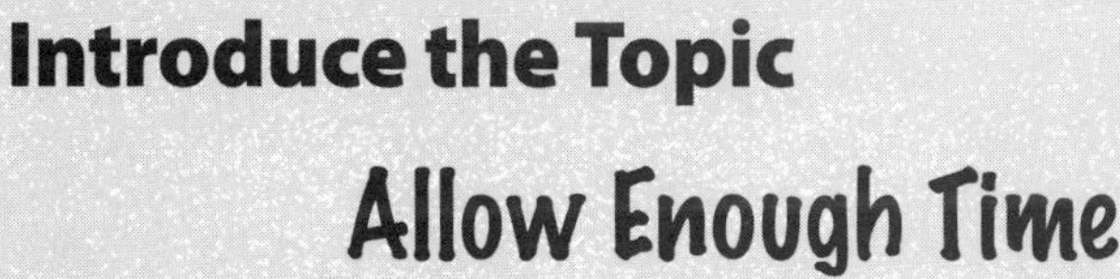

Introduce the Topic

Allow Enough Time

AFFIRM ALL RESPONSES—RIGHT OR WRONG

Don't Be the Authoritative Answer

LISTEN TO EACH PERSON

Don't Force It

Don't Take Sides

LET THEM LAUGH!

Allow Silence

BE CREATIVE AND FLEXIBLE

Be There for Your Kids

TalkSheet #39

DISCIPLESHIP

Your Life's Glue

1. What do the things on your personal bulletin board say about you?
(You may check more than one answer.)

- ❒ My life is pretty superficial.
- ❒ I need to rethink what to put on my bulletin board.
- ❒ When I look at my bulletin board I realize I have my life priorities straight.
- ❒ My life looks impressive.
- ❒ My life is a mess.
- ❒ Jesus would be impressed with what I placed on my bulletin board.
- ❒ Help!

2. Read Matthew 6:19-21. What is Jesus saying here? Put it in your own words. How does what Jesus is saying relate to what you have on your bulletin board? What is he asking you to do?

3. Super Glue or Temporary Stickiness? Go back to your bulletin board. Which of these do you feel might not be as important to you in one year, five years, or even 10 years? Which of these do you feel will be important to you next year, five years from now, or 10 years for now?

4. Rate from least true to most true (1 Most true to 5 Least true):

_____ Everything I do in life has lasting value.
_____ Some things I think are important are not.
_____ Some things are important only for a season.
_____ Everything in my life is of equal value to me.
_____ I have some things in my life that will always be important to me.

5. How can we tell the difference between those things that are temporary and those things that will last?

THIS WEEK

Consider how we prioritize the importance of events, objects, people, and activities in our lives. There are some things in our lives that are so important to us we might consider them "our life's glue"; in other words, these things can or might seem to "hold us together" by giving our lives purpose, meaning, context, energy. While it is important to never denigrate what is important to another person, this session is aimed at helping us realize we do hold things as important in our lives and that some things might be and might not be of lasting importance.

THE OPENER

Ask your group members to close their eyes. Tell them they are going to create a personal bulletin board. Pretend a piece of paper is a bulletin board in your room that hangs in a place where anyone could see it. If you were going to place things on this bulletin board that would tell anyone who sees it what is most important to your life right now, what holds your life together and gives it meaning and happiness, what would you place on the board? You must place no less than two objects and no more than six. Objects can be pictures, drawings, or other small items that represent people, moments, or things to you.

DISCUSSION BY THE NUMBERS (Go through the TalkSheet one item at a time.)

1. What was your group's most common response? The least common? What does this say about your group?
2. Have the young people get down to the important point Jesus is making. We make so many things important in our lives. Some things just aren't while there *are* some things that just are important. Ask, **What do you think was the glue in Jesus' life? How does what Jesus is saying here relate to what is on our bulletin boards? How are the things represented on your personal bulletin board your *life glue* (the things that hold your life together)?**
3. These questions dig deeper into **Matthew 6:19-21**. Ask, **What could happen to change what is important to you?**
4. These statements will not be rated in one way only. Depending on how we hear these statements, we will rate them differently. Hopefully the first statement will be rated as least truthful, but the rest will only create good conversation about what we value in life.
5. Make a verbal list of the answers to this question. Ask, **How are the things that will last related to our faith?**

CLOSING DISCUSSION

Everyone places value on others, on events or activities, upon objects and abilities. We might even over-identify ourselves with these things. Some things are for a lifetime. Some things are for a season. Jesus is not specific in Matthew, but he does raise the issue. If we are going to follow him, we must be aware that those things we value most might need to be of lasting value. Ask, **Why do you think Jesus wants us to give greater energy to those things that will last in our lives?**

CLOSING PRAYER

"Dear Father, we thank you for those people, activities, objects, and talents we have in our life that we enjoy, that we hold dear. May what we truly hold dear and give energy to be of lasting value to our relationship with you. Amen."

TalkSheet #40

THE BLOCK WHERE YOU LIVE

1. Read the Gospel of John 15:1-10. How many times does Jesus say either "abide in" or "remain in"? Why do you think Jesus says it so often?

2. A=Agree, D=Disagree. Circle A for agree and D for disagree.

a. To remain in Jesus one needs to go to church more often.	A	D
b. Jesus wants me to take him everywhere I go from now on.	A	D
c. In the church building is where people abide best.	A	D
d. To abide /remain in Jesus means I live into him and out of him daily.	A	D
e. The Bible is the only tool I have to help me abide.	A	D

3. Finish these Sparkplug Sentences:

By "abide," or "remain," I think Jesus means…

For me to "abide" in Jesus, I think I would have to…

One thing that would help me "remain in him" would be…

4. John 15:5 uses the image of a vine and branches. What is another image you could use to describe such a close relationship? (Pick the image you like best and explain why.)

- ❒ Banana trees with bunches of bananas
- ❒ A poison ivy patch with me in the middle
- ❒ Peanut butter, jelly, and two pieces of bread
- ❒ Book pages and the words written on the pages
- ❒ A guitar and strings
- ❒ A car and gasoline
- ❒ A wall in your house and a door
- ❒ Other ________________________________

5. Moving In! List two things you would do this week to move in with Jesus.

1. ________________________________

2. ________________________________

40. THE BLOCK WHERE YOU LIVE

THIS WEEK

In a culture where we tend to compartmentalize our relationships, it is easy to only see our relationship with Jesus as something we do in the church building or at special church gatherings. It is important that our relationship with Jesus takes place in all areas of our lives. Jesus seems to stress this as he speaks with his disciples in John 15:1-10. This week we want to have the young people consider how they might compartmentalize their relationships and consider the extent to which Jesus wants to be involved in their lives.

THE OPENER

Ask your group members to consider three areas of their lives: Home, school, and church. Ask them to consider two things they do only in those places. Allow your group members time to reflect and offer their answers. Then ask them to consider two things they do in all three places. Again, allow them time to answer. Ask: **Do we tend to act differently at home than at school, or differently at school than at church? Why is this?**

DISCUSSION BY THE NUMBERS (Go through the TalkSheet one item at a time.)

1. The emphasis Jesus gives to abiding or remaining in him suggests this as an important point Jesus is making to his followers. Ask, **Why do you think Jesus says it so often?** Allow time for reflection and answers.
2. This Agree/Disagree section provides an opportunity for your young people to consider how they see Jesus involved in every area of their lives. Select one side of the room to be Agree and the other for Disagree. Have the young people move to one side if they agree and the other if they disagree. Allow time to explore why they agree or disagree with the statements.
3. Ask your group members to respond to the incomplete sentences. These **Sparkplug Sentences** are designed to jumpstart discussion and have the group consider their day-to-day relationship with Jesus.
4. Ask your group members to share their images. Ask, **How does your image show your attachment to Jesus Christ?**
5. Ask your young people for two things they might do this week to move in with Jesus. This section is asking them to consider how they might bring their relationship with Jesus into all areas of their lives.

CLOSING DISCUSSION

Christians believe that Jesus calls us into a lifelong relationship into which and out of which we are to live our daily lives. To "abide," or remain, in him is to make our "home" in him. Most of what we do together as Christians when we gather is to strengthen that relationship through worship, prayer, Scripture, and service. Our relationship with Jesus is not a Sunday-only thing, but a relationship for every day of our lives. Ask, **Why do you think Jesus thought it was important that our relationship with him be in every part of our lives?** Then ask, **Why would you want more than a Sunday relationship with Jesus?**

CLOSING PRAYER

"Dear Lord, we know we live in a fragmented world. We have a tendency to act one way with our friends and another way with our family, one way in church and another way at home or school. But we hear you asking us to live with you the same way every place we go and the same no matter who we are with. Help us to remain with you in all areas of our lives. Amen."

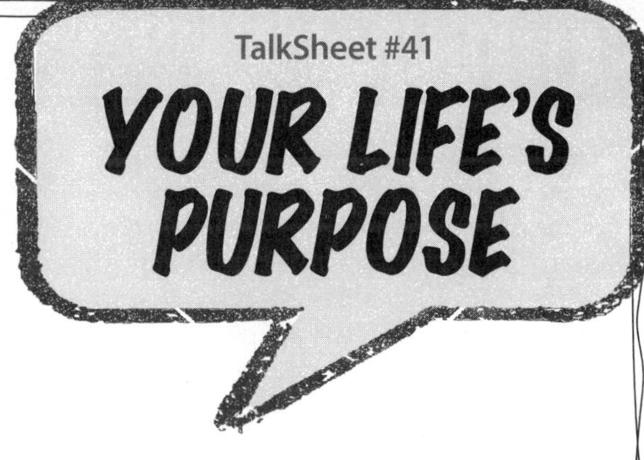

1. Rate the following on the "That's Why I'm Here" Scale:

1________2________3________4________5________
Not important Could be important

6________7________8________9________10________
Somewhat important Important

a. To have a good time
b. To train for a good career
c. To win friends and influence people
d. To make a difference in the world
e. To live out my life with dignity
f. To do something important
g. To get wealthy

2. Read Matthew 4:1-11. What was Jesus' response to the temptation to be relevant, to be popular, and to be powerful?

To be relevant Jesus responded—

To be popular Jesus responded—

To be powerful Jesus responded—

3. Finish these Sparkplug Sentences:

I believe my life's purpose is to be…

I want to use this gift of life to…

The most important thing I can do with my life is…

4. List any three things you remember Jesus telling us we need to be doing with our lives.

a. ____

b. ____

c. ____

5. Listen Three Times to this question and answer:

Q. What is the chief and highest end of man?
A. Man's chief and highest end is to glorify God, and to fully enjoy him forever.

1st Reading – What stands out to you?

2nd Reading – How does this connect with your world?

3rd Reading – What do you feel called to do in response?

41. YOUR LIFE'S PURPOSE

THIS WEEK
What is our life's purpose? What should I see as the highest claim upon my life? These are questions a young person hears answered in many ways in our culture. The church has wrestled with these questions, and through the Holy Spirit and through Scripture, has determined that our highest purpose in life is to know God and to demonstrate God in our living, enjoying the new and wonderful relationship we have through Jesus Christ. This realization of the church is so important to young people who need to understand that enjoying God is an essential part of our Christian experience.

THE OPENER
Ask, **What is one thing you really want to do with your life before you die?** This question introduces the idea that our lives can have a purpose and that we can live our lives intentionally in order to achieve the purpose we set for our lives.

DISCUSSION BY THE NUMBERS (Go through the TalkSheet one item at a time.)

1. Ask your young people for their ratings. See which of the activities rated the most important. Discuss.
2. Ask, **In what ways are you tempted to be relevant, popular, and powerful?**
3. Listen to the completed sentences. Refer any questions back to the group for consideration, allowing them to take a shot at the answers before you do.
4. Ask, **How does what Jesus said inform the purpose of your life?**
5. The answer came from the Westminster Larger Catechism. As you read it, ask the young people to respond following each reading to the corresponding question. Reference texts in the Bible can be found in **Romans 11:36, 1 Corinthians 10:31,** and **John 17:22, 24.**

CLOSING DISCUSSION
Christians believe we are called by God to live our lives intentionally and that the highest end or focus for our lives is to know God, to show God's love in and through how we live (glorify God), and to simply enjoy this relationship with God daily. We are created to enjoy life much like Adam and Eve, who walked daily in the garden with God. Ask, **In what ways could you live your life more intentionally to enjoy your relationship with God?**

CLOSING PRAYER
"Dear Father, you have given us the gift of life. It is ours to live each and every day. With so many voices trying to tell us what is important and how we should live, we really want to listen to you, to hear what you have to tell us about what IS important in living our lives. Above all, Father, as we live help us let our relationship with you show through to others in such a way that we have a good time doing it. Amen."

TalkSheet #42

WHAT IS FAITH AND DOES IT MATTER ANYWAY?

1. **Trust-O-Meter:** Rate the following by placing the letter on the meter.

   1________2________3________4________5________
   Nope Maybe

   6________7________8________9________10________
   I could You bet!!

   I can trust…
   a. A neighbor with my parent's car.
   b. A family member with a personal secret.
   c. My pastor with a family secret.
   d. A school friend with my homework for tomorrow.
   e. A teacher in a conference with your parents.

2. **Read Mark 2:1-12. What important thing did Jesus see in the paralyzed man and his friends? How did they demonstrate to Jesus they had this?**

3. **Finish these Sparkplug Sentences:**

   To have faith in God means I would…

   The hardest thing about faith for me is…

   Faith is important in a relationship with God because…

4. **Which of the following statements describes Faith (F) and which describes Doubt (D)?**

   ____ Thomas wanted to see it before he would believe it.
   ____ Abraham left his home not knowing where he was going.
   ____ Noah built an ark from gopher wood.
   ____ Judas went to the high priests and told them where Jesus would be.
   ____ Mary responded to the angel's news—"let this happen to me as you say."
   ____ A group of men tear a hole in a roof to get their paralyzed friend to Jesus.

5. **Listen to Hebrews 11:6. What does this tell us about faith? (Check as many as believe are true.)**

   ❒ You need it in your relationship with God.
   ❒ It believes that God is God.
   ❒ It counts on what God promises.
   ❒ Nothing pleases God more.
   ❒ It is something you know is not true but like believing anyway.
   ❒ Without it you and God have nothing to say to each other.
   ❒ It is the only way to get in good with God.

42. WHAT IS FAITH AND DOES IT MATTER ANYWAY?

THIS WEEK

Faith is an essential part of our relationship with God. Young people can misunderstand what faith is and how one lives in and out of their relationship with God. It is important to understand that what one has faith in is more important than how hard one believes. Faith needs to have a worthy recipient of our trust. We believe God has proven himself trustworthy throughout the ages and in the resurrection of Jesus. God is worthy of our trust and our faith.

THE OPENER

Begin by asking your young people to consider something in their lives they feel is trustworthy—something in their daily lives they trust to be dependable. The natural tendency may be to give a religious answer, but we would hope they might explore simple objects like a chair upon which they place their weight without thinking about it.

DISCUSSION BY THE NUMBERS (Go through the TalkSheet one item at a time.)

1. Take time to discuss each situation and explore why one does or does not trust.
2. Ask, **How do you think you demonstrate your faith in Christ? When have you demonstrated the most faith in Christ?**
3. After listening to volunteers read their completed sentences, read yours. Then, with the group, answer questions generated from the completed sentences.
4. The Faith/Doubt section asks the group to remember stories from Scripture and consider whether the person was acting on faith or doubt. Ask, **How do you know it was faith or doubt at work?**
5. Read the Bible text and ask your young people to discuss why each statement is or is not true.

CLOSING DISCUSSION

Christians believe it is by faith we are saved in Christ **(Romans 10:9-10)**. Faith is not about believing strongly. Rather it is about trusting the faithfulness of the one in whom you believe. You might believe strongly the ice in a river will hold you up. But if it is thin, it will break no matter how much you believe. Is the one you have faith in faithful and trustworthy? Christians believe God has "proved his love" trustworthy in Jesus and therefore we can put our faith in him. Ask, **How is faith more than merely thinking something is so?** Then ask, **Has God proven to you he is trustworthy?**

CLOSING PRAYER

"Dear Father, you ask us to put our trust in you, to believe you and to live like people who believe you. You ask us to have faith. Help us grow in faith and trust daily as we come to know you better in our lives. Amen."

TalkSheet #43

STEWARDSHIP

Minding God's Store

1. GIMME FIVE things you care for in your life that belong to another.

1. ______________________________
2. ______________________________
3. ______________________________
4. ______________________________
5. ______________________________

2. Read Matthew 25:14-30. What stands out for you in this reading? Check all that apply.

- ❒ We should all start a bank account as soon as possible.
- ❒ Some people get more and some people get less.
- ❒ Fear can cause us to do silly things with God's gifts.
- ❒ We need to be serious about how we tend God's gifts.
- ❒ I've got more than you've got!
- ❒ God cares about what we do with what he's given us.
- ❒ It's bad to bury a talent in the ground.

3. Finish these Sparkplug Sentences:

As a steward of God's stuff I think I need to…

When I think about having a relationship with Jesus, being his steward means to me that…

One thing about stewardship that comforts me is…

4. After reading Genesis 1:26-31 decide which of the following statements you (A) Agree with and (D) Disagree with.

a. A steward of God is what I was made to be.	A	D
b. God wants us to be involved in caring for the Earth.	A	D
c. One way we live as the image of God is to care.	A	D
d. God gave all of us everything but we own nothing.	A	D
e. To rule over everything means we decide what to do.	A	D

5. *African Bible Study* – Read Ephesians 4:11-16 three times, stopping each time to reflect.

1st Reading – What stands out to you?

2nd Reading – How does this connect with your world?

3rd Reading – What do you feel called to do in response?

43. STEWARDSHIP: Minding God's Store

THIS WEEK

Young people can get caught up in the passions of the consumer society and have difficulty in understanding the concept of stewardship beyond the simple act of tithing. Stewardship is an important concept in the Christian experience. The Bible makes it clear God has entrusted to all people the management and care of all creation. We are even to see ourselves as stewards of his gospel, his grace, his forgiveness, and his mercy as part of the body of Christ. Stewardship is an important aspect of our relationship with Jesus.

THE OPENER

Begin by asking your young people to consider and comment upon a time they were made responsible for another's property. Ask them to share their experience by sharing what they cared for, to whom it belonged, and what that experience was like. From here introduce the topic of stewardship as an important aspect of our relationship with Jesus.

DISCUSSION BY THE NUMBERS (Go through the TalkSheet one item at a time.)

1. Explore with your group what caring for another's property means to them.
2. An additional option and a good teaching experience would be to act out the story with your young people. Ask, **What was important in the relationship of each servant to his master in this story? How might you have that same kind of relationship with God?**
3. Listen to the completed sentences. Ask, **What was the most difficult part about completing the sentences?**
4. Use these Agree/Disagree statements to talk about **Genesis 1:26-31**.
5. Use this African Bible Study to discuss **Ephesians 4:11-16** with your group. Ask, **As stewards of the money, time, and abilities God has given you, how are you using them to help mature the church, the body of Christ?**

CLOSING DISCUSSION

Christians believe that all we have is from God and belongs ultimately to God. We enjoy, manage, share, and care for, for a time, what really is ours on loan. Good stewardship is the proper attitude toward and use of all that God has entrusted in our care. From talents to material goods, the hours of the day to the knowledge of his love and forgiveness, all are entrusted to our proper use and care. Giving tithes is only one way we express our understanding of stewardship. Ask, **What stands out for you most about stewardship? How have you been a good steward of your time? Your talent? Your money? Your pain?**

CLOSING PRAYER

"Dear Father, you are the Author of all things—all life, all talents, all creation. So often we can get caught up into thinking we own parts of your world and can do with it whatever we want. Help us to live in relationship with you in such a way that we enjoy the gift of life and the responsibility of being good stewards of what is ours for only a short time and what is yours forever: US. Amen."

TalkSheet #44

SABBATH

Keepin' It or Leapin' It?

1. **Gimme Five** of the most relevant things you do each week:

   1. ______________________________
   2. ______________________________
   3. ______________________________
   4. ______________________________
   5. ______________________________

2. Rate the following on the **"Being Relevant"** Scale:

   1____2____3____4____5____6____7____8____9____10
   Not relevant — Might be — Quite often is — VERY!!

   a. Spending time with my family
   b. Doing my homework
   c. Time with friends after school
   d. A daily devotional time
   e. Practicing my favorite sport or hobby
   f. Sunday mornings at my church
   g. A time for serious spiritual reflection and renewal
   h. Going to every one of my classes

3. **Read Exodus 20:8-11.** What does this passage have to do with your life? Choose one.

   - I live for the weekends.
   - I need to spend one day a week with God.
   - My week needs to have a rhythm that includes God.
   - There is a time to work and a time to not work.
   - I need to veg out more.
   - If God needs to rest, so do I.
   - The world has patterns I need to pay attention to.

4. Finish these **Sparkplug Sentences:**

   The hardest thing for me about keeping the Sabbath is…

   When it comes to taking Sabbath time with God, I find I…

   What seems right to me about keeping the Sabbath is…

5. **Three FOR/Three AGAINST:** List three forces in your life that make it hard to keep the Sabbath and three forces that could help you to keep the Sabbath:

HELP		MAKE IT HARD
____________	<< >>	____________
____________	<< >>	____________
____________	<< >>	____________

6. **African Bible Study:** As we think about keeping the Sabbath, read **Matthew 11:28** three times and respond following each reading.

   1st Reading – What stands out in this text for you?

   2nd Reading – How does this text relate to your life and keeping the Sabbath right now?

   3rd Reading – What do you feel you need to do in response to this text?

THIS WEEK

Keeping the Sabbath holy, or set apart, is a big issue in the current culture and today's church. There are many pressures and pulls through activities and commitments in young people's lives. Yet more and more the church is reconsidering how important a faithful rhythm of work and Sabbath is for life and for faith. It is important that we introduce to young people the essential Christian experience of keeping Sabbath time with God.

THE OPENER

Ask your group to call out the first thing they think of when they hear the word *Sabbath*.

DISCUSSION BY THE NUMBERS (Go through the TalkSheet one item at a time.)

1. This activity helps your group members consider how they live their lives each week, and what in their weeks are considered relevant activities for their lives. Everyone's definition of what is relevant can be different. The question may arise, "What does it mean to be relevant?" Encourage them to explore what is and what is not relevant in their daily lives.
2. This activity leads your group further into a discussion of what is relevant and meaningful in their daily lives. Explore what a time of spiritual reflection and renewal would look like. Talk about which of the items is the most Sabbath-like and which is the least.
3. Read the Bible text and ask your young people to discuss their choice of response.
4. Listen to the completed sentences. What themes are common among all your group members?
5. After listening to your group members' lists, ask, **Which side are you on?** or, **To which side do you give the most energy?**
6. Use the African Bible study to explore **Matthew 11:28.**

CLOSING DISCUSSION

Christians believe it is important to have a faithful rhythm of work and of Sabbath in one's week. The Sabbath is a day where you relax from the rush and the commitments and remember who you are and who God is in your life. Such a rhythm keeps a healthy balance and perspective in life and in faith. Ask, **How do you think keeping Sabbath time might be a relevant activity in your life?** Then ask, **How many of your friends keep a Sabbath? Your family members?**

CLOSING PRAYER

"Dear Father, you have given us life and this incredible world in which to live. It is so easy for us to get caught up in it all and rarely stop to remember who we are and who you are in our lives. You tell us to observe the Sabbath every week and to keep our time with you set apart from all other activities—to keep it special. Help us look at our lives and see how we can faithfully keep our times with you. Amen."

TalkSheet #45

PRAYER

Can WE Talk?

1. **URGENT PHONE CALL!** **Consider the following conversations and place the letter of the conversation on the "Phone Call Importance" Scale. With whom do YOU need to talk?**

   1________2________3________4________5________
   I'll call 'em back — Just a minute

   6________7________8________9________10________
   I'll take this one — So glad you called!

   a. A pollster wants to ask you about your mobile phone use.
   b. The president is on the line and wants to ask you a question.
   c. The lead singer of that boy band is calling.
   d. Your teacher has a question about your homework.
   e. The pastor is calling about this Sunday's sermon.
   f. Someone called "God" is on the line for you.
   g. That talent scout is calling again.

2. **Conversation Estimation**

   Estimate the number of times a week you talk with your friends (phone, text, email): _________.

   Estimate the number of minutes a week you talk with your friends: _________.

   Estimate the number of times a week you pray: _________.

   Estimate the number of minutes a week you pray: _________.

3. **Consider Psalm 5:1-3. What can the psalmist speak to God about? What does the psalmist know God does in response?**

4. **Finish these Sparkplug Sentences:**

   Prayer is one way I can…

   What I don't understand about prayer is…

   The important thing about prayer for me is…

5. **Gimme Five. Read Matthew 6:5-15 and list five important things to remember that Jesus tells YOU about prayer.**

   1. ______________________________________
   2. ______________________________________
   3. ______________________________________
   4. ______________________________________
   5. ______________________________________

45. PRAYER: Can WE Talk?

THIS WEEK

Prayer is an important aspect of our Christian experience. Young people often do not understand prayer and can struggle with how, when, and why one prays. This week the young people will consider conversation. It is important for young people to understand that prayer is above all an open and honest conversation between us and God made possible through our relationship with Jesus Christ.

THE OPENER

Ask the young people to consider one person they would really like to sit down with and talk to, and to consider what they would like to talk about. Allow each one time to reflect and offer answers.

DISCUSSION BY THE NUMBERS (Go through the TalkSheet one item at a time.)

1. See how your group members responded—which calls did they value and why? The purpose of this activity is to explore prayer as a conversation integral to the Christian life that we can have every day and everywhere.
2. Ask, **What is the longest period of time you've ever spent in prayer? The shortest period of time?** Compare God and friend conversation times and minutes. Ask, **What does this say about our face time with God?**
3. Ask, **How are you like or unlike the Psalmist?**
4. These sentences will generate questions about prayer. Take time to answer these questions together with your group members.
5. You may want to create a list on a whiteboard or flipchart paper of the things your group members want to remember.

CLOSING DISCUSSION

Christians believe that prayer is the essence of our experience with God. We know we can talk with God about anything and that we also need to listen as God speaks to us. Prayer is simply honest communication between us and God made possible because of Jesus. It is our way of being intimate with God and God's way of being intimate with us. Ask, **Why is prayer so important that Jesus would take time to teach us about it?**

CLOSING PRAYER

"Dear Father, thank you that you long to listen to us and that you long for us to listen to you. You want to be in conversation with us every day and at any time. And we know you tell us we can talk with you about anything. Father, help us see how precious the opportunity is to speak with you at any time. Amen."

TalkSheet #46

OBEDIENCE

To Hear and to Do

1. The "It Really Matters When . . ." Scale: Rate the importance of obedience in the following situations, from when it matters least to when it matters most by placing the appropriate letter on the scale.

1________2________3________4________5________
Hardly Well, yeah

6________7________8________9________10________
Oh, my You bet!!

a. Your dog is loose and running toward the busy street.
b. Your parents told you to be in at midnight, but you want to stay out until 1 a.m.
c. The question is hard and the teacher warned about cheating, but if you stretch you can see someone else's answer.
d. The Bible says, "Do not steal," but it's just gum…and you have no money.
e. The sign says, "Take only one, please," but you love doughnuts!
f. The sign says the speed limit is 35 mph, but you're late for school.

2. Read Matthew 21:28-30. How is obedience about *hearing* and *doing*? (Check the one that best relates to you and this reading.)

- ❐ You need to do what you say you will do.
- ❐ You do what you were asked to do.
- ❐ What another doesn't know won't hurt you.
- ❐ Tell someone what they want to hear.
- ❐ Obeying God is more than lip service.
- ❐ It matters what we do in response to what we hear.
- ❐ Parents always ask too much of us anyway.

3. A=Agree, D=Disagree. Circle A for agree and D for disagree.

a. Doing anything is okay as long as you don't get caught.	A	D
b. To obey is to do something you're told even when you don't want to.	A	D
c. Obedience is important to God because it is about relationship.	A	D
d. Obedience is not as important today as it was in Bible times.	A	D
e. If I want to get close to Jesus, I need to know what he wants and do it.	A	D

4. Ask, When do you feel the most obedient toward God? The most rebellious?

5. Listen to John 15:12-15. How does obedience play an important role in being Jesus' friend? (Check one or more responses.)

- ❐ It's the difference between being a friend and a servant.
- ❐ He laid down his life for us, so we should be grateful.
- ❐ Friends of Jesus do what he asked them to do.
- ❐ Obedience is the only right response to Jesus.
- ❐ I'm not sure, but let me get back to you on this.
- ❐ Jesus has let us in on everything God is up to, so why not?
- ❐ A friend wouldn't ask you to obey him.

46. OBEDIENCE: To Hear and to Do

THIS WEEK

Obedience is not a popular subject today. The culture's thinking is aimed for the most part at self-determination and relativity. Little is made of being obedient and submissive to God's will over *our* will. Young people need to see how important obedience is in any relationship. The root of the word *obedience* means "to hear, and to do according to what you hear." The opposite of obedience is not disobedience but deafness. People live deaf lives when they neither hear nor act in response to their real relationships and surroundings. To be obedient is to know who you are and whose you are.

THE OPENER

Ask, **To whom are you most obedient?** to get your discussion about obedience going.

DISCUSSION BY THE NUMBERS (Go through the TalkSheet one item at a time.)

1. Explore how relationships and consequences play a role in deciding how important it is to have obedience in each situation.
2. Discuss their responses. In this parable the rebellious son (representing sinners whose natural response is to say no to God) changes his mind and obeys his father. The "obedient" son (representing the outwardly religious) disobeys. Jesus' lesson here? We must both hear Jesus and act on what Jesus says. This is true obedience.
3. Ask the young people to consider each statement in the Agree/Disagree section and, as you read the question, to take sides by walking to one side of the room or the other. Take time to explore each statement and ask why the young people agree or disagree with it.
4. Have each of your young people consider the question and offer a time when they feel most obedient and when they might feel most disobedient.
5. Read the Bible text then discuss their response and why it is true for them. Ask, **Why does Jesus say he now calls us friends? What does he say we need to do to be his friend? Why is that important to him?**

CLOSING DISCUSSION

Christians believe obedience is important in our experience. We believe it is not about dos and don'ts, as much as it is about our relationship with God and each other and about living in a loving manner in our world. The heart of obedience is about understanding our relationships, with God and one another, and living in a way that obeys the need of the moment: To love above all things. We obey, we hear, and we obey God's commands, because we know that all his commands are about love. Read **Psalm 32:9** and ask, **How are you like the horse and mule in this verse in your relationship with God? How are you not like them?**

CLOSING PRAYER

"Dear Father, loving Lord, sometimes it seems as though there is so much we are supposed to do, so many rules, so many dos and don'ts in this relationship with you. And so often we just want to do our own thing and not bother with rules. But that is because we don't understand you, and we don't trust your love for us. Help us to hear your voice, to trust your love, and when we hear, to live our lives in faithful response to what we hear. Amen."

SECTION 8 QUESTIONS ABOUT KEY WORDS OF FAITH

If you put these instructions before the brothers and sisters, you will be a good servant of Christ Jesus, nourished on the words of the faith and of the sound teaching that you have followed. (1 Timothy 4:6 NRSV)

Introduce the Topic

Allow Enough Time

AFFIRM ALL RESPONSES—RIGHT OR WRONG

Don't Be the Authoritative Answer

LISTEN TO EACH PERSON

Don't Force It

Don't Take Sides

LET THEM LAUGH!

Allow Silence

BE CREATIVE AND FLEXIBLE

Be There for Your Kids

1. **Rate the following on the "Gotta Pass It On" Scale by placing the letter on the line.**

1________2________3________4________5________
Forget It! Might Mention It

6________7________8________9________10________
Worth Telling Check This Out!

a. A good movie
b. A new music group
c. An exciting television show
d. A joke
e. Youth group meeting
f. A cheap pizza place

2. **Read Luke 4:16-20. Is this the Good News? (Check one or more responses.)**

- Jesus got to sit down when he was finished reading.
- It is something everyone was waiting for.
- Jesus was saying this Bible promise was coming true because of him.
- Jesus got to go to the synagogue, as was his custom.
- People in prison will be freed and people who are blind will be made to see.
- Jesus is proclaiming that the year of God's favor has arrived.
- Jesus is saying the oppressed people will be released.

3. **Finish these Sparkplug Sentences:**

For me something is good news when it…

To me the Good News (the gospel) is about…

For me to pass something on it has to be…

4. **Read 1 John 1:1-4. John is excited about sharing the life-giving Word, Jesus Christ. Why do you think Jesus is the One who gives life? How is this life given? Who gets to receive this life? How will they hear about this new life?**

5. **What do you find is the most difficult about sharing the Good News with others? The easiest?**

47. THE GOSPEL: What's So Good about Its News?

THIS WEEK
There are many voices in our culture that speak excitedly about so many things that the church's proclamation of "Good News!" might seem to get lost in the crowd. Young people are used to sharing with one another "good news" about movies, music, people, etc. Sometimes young people are not clear about what makes news good and what it means to "pass it on." In this session we open up conversation about what makes news good and why anyone might want to share it with someone else.

THE OPENER
Begin the discussion by asking your young people to consider a recent time when they wished to share something with someone else. Ask the young people to talk about what they shared (being careful to observe any confidentialities) and with whom they shared it. Then explore with each one the reason behind his or her desire to share by asking, **Why did you want to share that with someone else?**

DISCUSSION BY THE NUMBERS (Go through the TalkSheet one item at a time.)

1. Ask the young people to rate the items listed on the "Gotta Pass It On" Scale by placing the letter on the scale according to how likely they would be to pass this on to someone else. Allow the young people to record their responses and then explore those.
2. Use this item to talk about what the Good News really is. Use the offered statements as a springboard for a discussion about what makes the Good News good news.
3. Listen to the completed sentences. Then try to answer the questions that arise from these sentences.
4. Talk about why Jesus, the life-giving Word, excited John so much. Remember, John, as a disciple, spent about three years with Jesus. Ask, **How does spending time with Jesus get you excited about sharing the Good News?**
5. Young and old alike in the church often find it difficult to share the Good News with their friends and relatives. Ask, **Why do you think people will talk about a good movie they saw over the weekend but shy away from talking about Jesus?**

CLOSING DISCUSSION
Christians believe that the message about Jesus is Good News, or gospel. What God has done through Jesus Christ is news worth hearing and worth sharing. In a world of so many uncertainties, it is good news to hear that God loves us AND has acted decisively upon that love to be in relationship with us. The Christian experience is about sharing the Good News. Ask, **How might the world hear about the Good News of Jesus in bad ways? How can we prevent that in the way we relate to people?**

CLOSING PRAYER
"Dear Lord, you have entered our lives, expressing your undying love for us and your desire to walk with us every day. We don't have to do anything to earn your love or fix that which we have no way of fixing. In this world of uncertainties, that IS good news—perhaps the best news of all. Help us to understand and know how incredible sharing that news can be. Amen."

TalkSheet #48

GRACE

Undeserved Favor

1. Rate the following on the "I Deserve This" Scale:

1________2________3________4________5________
Not at all — Not sure

6________7________8________9________10________
Most likely — You bet I do!

a. The air I breathe.
b. My parents' love.
c. A car on graduation.
d. Good grades in school.
e. The respect of my peers.
f. Food three times a day.

2. Read Matthew 20:1-16 and respond to the following:

What angers you in this parable?

What amazes you in this parable?

What gives you hope in this parable?

3. A=Agree, D=Disagree. Circle A for agree and D for disagree.

a. Most people deserve what they get in life.	A	D
b. God will reward you for what you do in life.	A	D
c. Sin always has consequences.	A	D
d. If someone says she's sorry, she deserves forgiveness.	A	D
e. Life should always be fair.	A	D

4. Finish these Sparkplug Sentences:

The important thing to me about grace is that I know…

When I hear about God's grace I feel…

If it were not for grace in life I would…

5. Read John 1:16-17. In what ways have you received one blessing after another because of Jesus? (Check one or more boxes.)

- ❒ I get to meet really nice people at church.
- ❒ I've got some really nice stuff in my room.
- ❒ God's forgiveness is available to me every single day.
- ❒ Life itself is a blessing and every day is icing on the cake.
- ❒ Being saved has changed the way I live every day.
- ❒ I wish I had a good response to that question.
- ❒ There are too many blessings in my life to count.

48. GRACE: Undeserved Favor

THIS WEEK
Grace is a difficult notion for most Christians to understand. Our culture tends toward emphasizing people getting what they deserve. But the heart of the Christian faith is not about fairness or what we deserve, but rather about God's freedom and desire to give us what in his mercy he gives us: Love. Grace is about undeserved favor, and young people need to hear the Good News of grace that surrounds them every day.

THE OPENER
Begin by asking the young people to consider a time when they either received or witnessed another receiving something they did not deserve. A negative example, such as when someone was punished unfairly, can also serve the discussion and lead to an exploration of unfairness in life. Take time to explore with your young people the experience of not getting what one deserves. Then lead into grace by stating, **As we talk about unfairness and not getting what one deserves, if we think on the positive side, we begin to get an idea of what grace is all about. How is grace about undeserved favor?**

DISCUSSION BY THE NUMBERS (Go through the TalkSheet one item at a time.)

1. This activity will get your group talking about what's deserved and not deserved. Push your group members to think beyond their world to the larger world and how grace works in that larger world.
2. The three questions can help you dig deeper into this parable of grace.
3. These Agree/Disagree statements will generate a lively discussion. Remember, today's TalkSheet discussion is all about grace—God's undeserved kindness!
4. These sentences will generate questions you can answer together with your group members.
5. Take time to discuss each response and why it speaks for them.

CLOSING DISCUSSION
Christians believe that forgiveness through Jesus and the new standing we have with God is all undeserved favor. Understanding grace is important in the Christian experience because it gives us a new outlook, attitude, and hope with which to live each day. Ask, **Why do you feel that understanding grace is an important part of the Christian experience?**

CLOSING PRAYER
"Dear Father, whose mercy and grace surrounds us every day of our lives, help us to get a sense of how much you have given us—because you love us and not because we have in any way earned your love or favor given us in Jesus Christ. For all you have given us—help us to be truly filled with thanksgiving. Amen."

TalkSheet #49

HOPE

1. **A=Agree, D=Disagree. Circle A for agree and D for disagree.**

a. Hope is about wanting something unlikely.	A	D
b. Hope is about looking forward to an unlikely possibility.	A	D
c. Hope is all about chance.	A	D
d. Hope is a desperate act of longing.	A	D
e. Hope desires something certain.	A	D
f. Hope means different things to different people.	A	D

2. **Read Romans 8:24-25. What do you think Paul really wants you to remember about hope? (Check one or more boxes.)**

- ❒ It's somewhere over the rainbow for me.
- ❒ Like faith, it's believing what I know isn't true.
- ❒ Hope in God's promises is something we wait patiently for.
- ❒ What we see is nothing compared with what's coming.
- ❒ I can set my heart on what God has promised us.
- ❒ I should be afraid to hope too much for fear of getting hurt.
- ❒ God has saved us as a hope for the whole world.

3. **Finish these Sparkplug Sentences:**

Hope to me is all about…

What **Psalm 39:7** means to me is…

One thing I expect I can count on because of Jesus is…

5. **Name one hope offered to us in the Bible.**

6. **African Bible Study** – Read **Ephesians 1:17-18** three times, stopping each time to reflect.

1st Reading – What stands out to you?

2nd Reading – How does this connect with your world?

3rd Reading – What do you feel called to do in response?

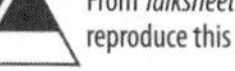

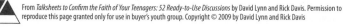

49. HOPE

THIS WEEK

Hope is a big part of the Christian experience and our relationship with God as we look forward to the promises of God. Yet our culture expresses hope with less emphasis on expectation and more on longing for personal desires that may be unrealistic. Youth are often confused about the nature of hope as they experience it in their culture. They experience a hope that is self-directed, feeble, and desperate in nature. But the Bible expresses hope as a power that transforms our daily living in the sure expectation of the fulfillment of the promises of God.

THE OPENER

Begin by asking your group members to consider and discuss a time when they (or someone they know) said, "I hope that…" Everyone says this at one time or another. *Hope* in our everyday culture is a word that has little depth and yet is used over-indulgently. Allow a few moments for everyone to consider responses.

DISCUSSION BY THE NUMBERS

(Go through the TalkSheet one item at a time.)

1. These statements can really jumpstart your discussion on hope. Give each young person the opportunity to share his or her opinion.
2. Read the Bible text and ask your young people to talk about the response that best states what they feel Paul would have them remember from his words. Discuss why they chose that response.
3. You'll definitely get questions based on these sentences. Throw the questions back to the group. If a question can't be answered, challenge your group members to ask your pastor or other congregation leader the question.
4. Ask each to name one hope offered to us out of the Bible. Allow struggle. The point is that everyone can share one thought on this topic, even if it is not correct. Ask, **Why is this sort of Christian hope different from the hope the world offers you?**
5. Use this African Bible study as a time to dig deeper into the meaning of Ephesians 1:17-18.

CLOSING DISCUSSION

Christians believe we can live in confident expectation of what God will do for us through Jesus Christ. God has "proved" his love for us in Jesus and has demonstrated his faithfulness to his promises. God's ability to fulfill what he has promised is something for which we can be filled with hope. Hope to Christians is not about chance, possibilities, or what could be. Hope is a firm conviction that what God has promised will come to pass. To be filled with hope is to live now in a confident relationship to what is to come. Ask, **In what way is hope an important part of the Christian experience?**

CLOSING PRAYER

"Dear Father, you have reached out to us in love and have promised so much to us that will be accomplished in Jesus Christ our Lord. We live in a world that fills us with longing for so much and yet offers us so little real hope we can count on. Only in you can we be confident we can really count on what you have promised. Thank you for your faithfulness to us always. Amen."

TalkSheet #50

DOUBT

1. Rate the following on the "I'm REALLY Sure" Scale.

I________2________3________4________5________
Not at all Somewhat

6________7________8________9________10________
Mostly REALLY Sure

a. Doubt is a dangerous thing.
b. Faith is trusting something you're not sure about.
c. There's a difference between doubt and disbelief.
d. Doubt displeases God.
e. The church should not have doubters.
f. Even doubters can believe.

2. Do you believe God is big enough to handle your doubts? (Check the one that speaks best for you.)

❏ I doubt it.
❏ God has a hard time touching me through my doubts.
❏ God doesn't teach me everything at once.
❏ Doubt angers God, so I need to pretend I believe.
❏ I am not sure, but I hope so.
❏ Doubt is "out" with a "duh" in the beginning.
❏ God's love covers everything.

3. Read James 1:6-8. When I hear James' words about doubt, it makes me think I should… (Check one or more.)

❏ Worry more.
❏ Doubt my doubts.
❏ Not be a wave on the sea.
❏ Settle my mind about my faith in Jesus.
❏ Pretend so God is pleased.
❏ Learn more about what God says in the Bible.
❏ Have listened more in Sunday school.

4. Finish these Sparkplug Sentences:

I find I doubt most…

I struggle with doubt when I think about…

What troubles me most about doubt is…

5. African Bible Study – Read Matthew 14:25-31 three times, stopping each time to reflect.

1st Reading – What stands out to you?

2nd Reading – How does this connect with your world?

3rd Reading – What do you feel called to do in response?

THIS WEEK

Doubt is a big issue in the lives of young people as they struggle with their faith and their daily lives in family, school, and friends. Often guilt can associate doubt with a desire to express certainty when uncertainty lingers. It is important that young people understand the nature of doubt and how it plays in faith development. Also the Bible presents many examples of those who struggled with doubt concerning God's ability and faithfulness—and who still lived out lives of faith and hope. The Psalms are filled with words of honest expression that questions and doubts. It is important to see doubt honestly as an experience while avoiding defining your life by paralysis and a lack of commitment.

THE OPENER

Begin by asking your group to consider and discuss a time when they found it hard to believe something or trust someone. Ask, **What were your reasons for lack of trust or doubt?**

DISCUSSION BY THE NUMBERS (Go through the TalkSheet one item at a time.)

1. Ask, **What are the reasons you are most sure about your highest rating?**
2. James knows that Jesus is more than good and stands ready to give us what we need. But we often lack the faith necessary to rely on Christ to provide for us.
3. Read the Bible text and ask your young people to talk about which response best speaks for them. Then discuss their responses.
4. Listen to the completed sentences. Do your best to answer questions that arise.
5. Use this African Bible study as a way to talk about Jesus walking on water and the disciples' terrified response.

CLOSING DISCUSSION

Christians believe that doubt is not incompatible with faith when we consider Thomas, who refused to believe until he saw with his own eyes, or Peter, who stepped out of the boat in trust. They are each an example of the struggle to understand and come to terms with faith in Christ. At the same time people can define their lives by doubt as a mark of the age, and to question all for the sake of being wishy-washy is a lack of commitment. While God does not honor a divided heart, he does not turn his back on one who seeks, asks, and knocks. Ask, **Why is doubt a part of the Christian experience?**

CLOSING PRAYER

"Dear Father, we do believe and yet there is that part in all of us that struggles to believe, that still doubts. We know you call us to faith and to hope. Like Peter, we want to walk out on the water with you. Like Thomas, we want to settle it all once and for all. 'Til everything is finally clear, walk with us, speak to our hearts, and lead us from doubt to find a sure hope in you. Amen."

TalkSheet #51

BORN AGAIN?

1. Read John 3:1-8. What do you think your friends would say if they heard the words *born again*?

- ❑ Could never happen.
- ❑ Yuck!
- ❑ I don't get it.
- ❑ Sounds hard.
- ❑ That's scientifically impossible.
- ❑ I'm ready for a change.
- ❑ That's me.

2. A=Agree, D=Disagree. Circle A for agree and D for disagree.

a. Being born again is different from believing in Jesus.	A	D
b. There are particular signs when one is born again.	A	D
c. Being born again is about what we do in response to Jesus.	A	D
d. Being born again is a natural part of accepting Jesus.	A	D
e. Being born again helps me to accept Jesus.	A	D
f. Every real believer is born again.	A	D

3. Finish these Sparkplug Sentences:

To me being born again means…

When someone is born by the Spirit, they are…

What confuses me about being born again is…

The coolest part of being born again is…

4. Read John 1:12-13. What important point do you believe John is making here?

- ❑ Some receive him, some don't.
- ❑ Those who receive him become children of God.
- ❑ We are not made children of God by our own efforts.
- ❑ Receiving Jesus into our lives is important.
- ❑ Humans decide if they want to be God's children or not.
- ❑ Being God's children is a different kind of birth.
- ❑ Our efforts do not match God's action.

5. Rate the following on the "Really Important to Know" Scale.

1________2________3________4________5________6________7________8________9________10________

Not really — Kinda — Important — Don't forget it!

a. Knowing the right stuff about the Bible
b. Knowing the right people at school
c. Knowing Jesus
d. Knowing what your future will hold
e. Knowing how to give change for a dollar
f. Knowing your best friend's mobile phone number

THIS WEEK

Being born again is an important topic whenever we consider the Christian experience. Many different Christian traditions relate to this topic with different emphasis. It is important to allow young people to explore this scriptural truth and understand it as a wonderfully natural part of the Christian tradition.

THE OPENER

Begin today's discussion by asking your young people to share a family story about their own births. Some of them may have elaborate stories while others may not have much to share. Be sure to honor each telling even if it as simple as when it happened and where. The important notion is that we all had a beginning and a time for being born that is unique to each of us. Ask, **What is unique in all of these stories, and what is common about all of these stories?** Allow ample time to explore with the group the uniqueness of our own births and the single similarity that we all enter this life. From here you might then ask, **What is unique, and what is common about us as followers of Jesus?**

DISCUSSION BY THE NUMBERS (Go through the TalkSheet one item at a time.)

1. This item gives you a fun way to jumpstart your conversation about being "born again"!
2. The term *born again* has become a cliché that carries baggage that these Agree/Disagree statements can help your group discuss.
3. Listen to the completed sentences. Make a note of the different questions that arise as your group listens to the completed sentences. Together, as a group, try to answer the questions.
4. Read the Bible text and ask your young people to talk about which responses they believe are true. Discuss which are and which are not true and why.
5. This activity allows you to see "knowing Jesus" within the context of other important things to know. Ask, **Why do you think "knowing Jesus" must be at the top of the Important Things to Know list?**

CLOSING DISCUSSION

Christians are often confused about what being born again means, and yet we all believe that it is an important way in which God acts in the life of one who believes in Jesus Christ. Christians believe that God's Spirit moves in us to birth us into a new life with God through Christ. That new life is being born again. Ask, **How is being born again important to you in your Christian experience today?**

CLOSING PRAYER

"Dear Father, we know we have entered a special relationship with you because of Jesus Christ. We know we can all call you Father because as followers of Jesus we are all your children. We thank you that through mystery we are filled with your Spirit and brought into your family as brothers and sisters. Thank you that in Jesus we are born again into a life full of hope. Amen."

TalkSheet #52

SPIRITUALITY

It's What You Lean Into

1. Rate the following statements on the "I Live Here" Scale. Place the letter of the statement on the scale from high to low according to where it stands for you.

1________2________3________4________5________
Not me! Somewhat

6________7________8________9________10________
More like it Really ME!

a. Following my favorite rock band.
b. Reading the weekly gossip sheets about celebrities.
c. Knowing what my favorite sports team is up to today.
d. Wanting to hear what the topic for Sunday is about.
e. Finding out the latest trend in fashion.
f. Learning more Bible verses by heart.
g. Following the plot of a great television show.

2. Read Luke 10:38-42. What point is this reading trying to express to you?

- ❑ I need to spend more time in the kitchen.
- ❑ Martha was a busybody and should have minded her own business.
- ❑ We can get too caught up in what does not matter in life.
- ❑ Spending time with Jesus really matters.
- ❑ Mary needs to get up and help from time to time.
- ❑ It's easy to get distracted and miss what we really need to be doing.
- ❑ The choices we make can make a big difference.

3. Finish these Sparkplug Sentences:

To me, being spiritual means…

What I'd like to know about spirituality is…

What concerns me most about my spiritual life is…

4. A=Agree, D=Disagree. Consider the following and decide if you agree or disagree with the statements.

a. Spiritual people are calmer than ordinary people.	A	D
b. Spirituality is not as important as Bible knowledge.	A	D
c. Spirituality isn't for everyone.	A	D
d. Spirituality makes people different.	A	D
e. All Christians are spiritual people.	A	D

5. Read Matthew 5:6. This verse is a good explanation of *spirituality*. How does this verse relate to your world? (Check one or more.)

- ❑ I long to have a better relationship with God.
- ❑ Spirituality is confusing to me.
- ❑ Going to church satisfies a deep need in me.
- ❑ It's a blessing to grow closer to God.
- ❑ Now that you mention it, I *am* hungry and thirsty.
- ❑ There's more to life than food and drink.
- ❑ I need to get hungrier about my faith.

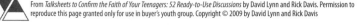

52. SPIRITUALITY: It's What You Lean Into

THIS WEEK
Spirituality is a buzzword in our culture. The mistake is to believe that only certain people are spiritual. Actually everyone is spiritual in that we all lean into something we believe, in such a way that belief takes concrete shape in our lives. The question is whether what we lean into is a cultural belief or trend, or a relationship with Jesus Christ. Young people can misunderstand the nature of spirituality because of how it is presented in culture. This session is designed to create conversation about spirituality from a Christian perspective.

THE OPENER
Begin by asking your young people to consider an area of their lives where they put most of their energies. This might be physical energy, as in sports, or emotional and mental energies as in following the lives of celebrities. Ask, **Why is it important to you? In what ways do you put your efforts into it?**

DISCUSSION BY THE NUMBERS (Go through the TalkSheet one item at a time.)

1. Ask the young people to share their ratings. This activity gets your group members thinking about where they put their energies. Say, **Let's talk more about spirituality today so we can place more of our time and energy into it!**
2. This story of Mary and Martha reflects two people in Jesus' presence who demonstrate what's important to them through where they focus their energies.
3. Answer together as a group the questions that arise from these sentences.
4. Ask the group members to consider the following statements and decide if they agree or disagree with the statements. After all have finished with their responses, have them respond to each statement by taking sides in the room. Then explore with two or three young people the reasoning behind their responses. Note that while their responses may be the same, the reasoning behind their responses may vary. Explore these differences with the group.
5. Read the Bible text and ask your youth to talk ab out one response that speaks best for them after hearing this text. Take time to discuss why this text speaks for them.

CLOSING DISCUSSION
Christians believe that spirituality is about the ways we are encountered by and lean into our relationship with God through Jesus Christ. Through the content of our character, the focus of our conduct, the nature of the community we bind ourselves to, the commitments we make, and the compassions we express, we bear witness to what we live in relationship to each day of our lives. That focus is our spirituality, which takes concrete shape in our daily lives. Ask, **How does spirituality relate to our Christian experience?**

CLOSING PRAYER
"Dear Father, you desire to be in relationship with us. There is so much in our lives that asks for our attention and demands our time. We put so much effort into what might be of little importance in the long run. Help us to discover how we might lean deeper into you every day. Amen."

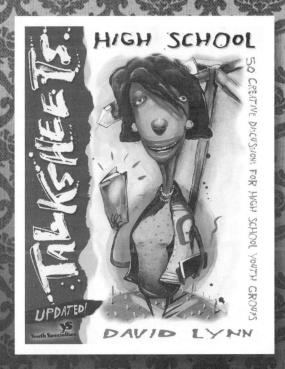

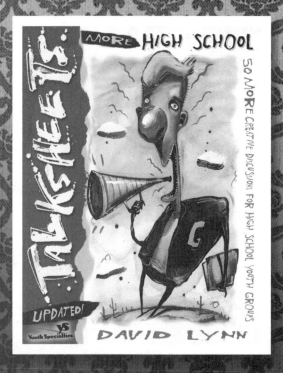

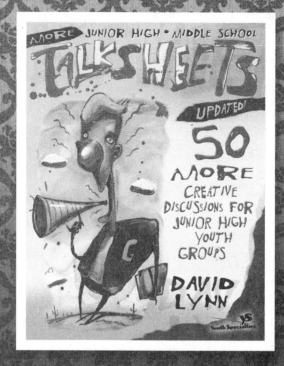

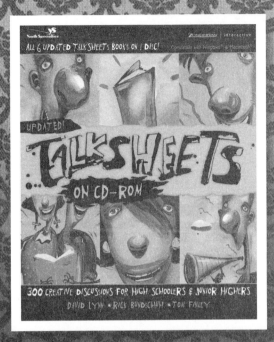